CORIOLANUS

CORIOLANUS

William Shakespeare

WORDSWORTH CLASSICS

This edition published 1996
by Wordsworth Editions Limited
Cumberland House, Crib Street, Ware,
Hertfordshire SG12 9ET

ISBN 1 85326 285 4

*Printed and bound in Great Britain
by Mackays of Chatham plc, Chatham, Kent*

INTRODUCTION

Coriolanus is believed to be Shakespeare's last tragedy. It was probably written c.1608, and was published in the first folio of 1623. The story of the 5th century Roman hero derives from Plutarch's *Life of Caius Martius Coriolanus*, and unlike other Roman plays by Shakespeare such as *Julius Cæsar* or *Antony and Cleopatra*, it was not a tale that was widely known to Elizabethans. It is an unusual and controversial play and, though never the most popular of Shakespeare's tragedies, *Coriolanus* has been considered by some critics to be among his finest works. T.S. Eliot, who wrote two poems linked by the title *Coriolan*, called it 'with *Antony and Cleopatra*, Shakespeare's most assured artistic success'.

The play presents the story of Caius Martius, a proud Roman General who is given the title of Coriolanus after taking the town of Coroli in a war against the marauding Volscians. In spite of his victory and triumphant return to Rome, Coriolanus cannot stoop to flatter the citizens, who are on the verge of rebellion. His arrogant disdain alienates him, and he is ultimately banished from the city. In revenge, Coriolanus leads the Volscians against the Romans, but is dissuaded from destroying his own city by the eloquent pleading of his mother, Volumnia. Back in Atrium the Volscian leader Aufidius has Coriolanus publicly executed for this betrayal.

The timeless theme of the individual in relation to society dominates the action, but in this stark political tragedy, Shakespeare observes the claims of the people on those who rule them with unusual concern. This preoccupation links the play more obviously with *King Lear* than to the other tragedies, but the very spare attention given to the story of the title figure himself suggests an affinity to *Timon of Athens* which was probably the next play that Shakespeare wrote.

The Roman plebeians are a constant force in the play, where imagery of disease is used consistantly to underline the social problems in Rome. Initially they are assuaged by Menenius Agrippa, the practised, smoothed-tongued politician whose celebrated speech likens the troubled state to a human body whose members (the citizens) rebel against its belly (the senators) to their own detriment (Act I sc.i). Their grievances are soon revived by the searing scorn of Coriolanus. An interesting contrast is drawn between these two patrician figures. The very qualities that have made Coriolanus victorious as a military leader are his undoing in peace-time. His hubristic belief in his own supremecy and his natural aggression cause him to fight everything he comes across in sharp disparity with the subtle, persuasive manipulations of Menenius. Such irony pervades the play, in Coriolanus' objection to the vacillations of the plebeians and his own subsequent behaviour, and particularly in the sight of Volumnia, who embodies the most arrogant patrician qualities and has made her son Coriolanus what he is, deterring him from wreaking his revenge.

Coriolanus is not a sympathetic character but he is an extreme product of his class. The general rudeness of the patricians to the plebians (who are not, however, idealized) is seen beside their courtesy to each other. Coriolanus suffers from a complete lack of self-knowledge, from which stems his inability to comprehend or handle others. His tragedy is that he cannot develop in the way that even his mother does. Outside the city walls, he defers to Volumnia because she is his mother rather than because he has made the moral leap. He never reaches a perception of the virtue in peacemaking or of the possibility of redemption. Aufidius taunts Coriolanus before his death with being a boy, and this is not unfounded. In *Coriolanus*, the failings of human nature point to the qualities essential to wholeness in life.

Shakespeare's verse in *Coriolanus* is compressed yet flexible in the manner that has come to be associated with his maturity. It is a play that can be mounted to reflect very different political attitudes. To the Victorians, Coriolanus was an Imperialist, but in 1933 a Paris production which presented the central character as an unblemished saviour was brought to a close by angry mobs. Berthold Brecht wrote a Marxist version of the play for the Berliner Ensemble which emphasized the dispensability of any leader. Shakespeare's text probes the integrity of the state while illustrating the frustrations of democracy, stressing the rights of both citizens and leaders with characteristic ambivalence. He gives the play universal implications in his portrayal of a man missing his achievements in the belief that he is irreplaceable, and in the suggestion of the beneficent aspects of the state, subtly presented as an extension of the family in Cominius' speech to the plebs (Act III sc.iii).

The political and military themes, the rich ironies and exciting story have made *Coriolanus* popular with modern audiences. Its battle scenes are invariably spectacular in production, and the play offers a challenging prospect for any director. The quality of its verse and the special interest afforded by this unusual study of social influence make this one of Shakespeare's most rewarding plays.

Details of Shakespeare's early life are scanty. He was born the son of a prosperous merchant of Stratford-upon-Avon, and tradition has it that he was born on 23rd April 1564; records show that he was baptized three days later. It is likely that he attended the local grammar school, but he had no university education. Of his early career there is no record, though John Aubrey states that he was, for a time, a country schoolmaster. How he became involved with the stage is equally uncertain, but he was sufficiently established as a playwright by 1592 to be criticised in print. He was a leading member of the Lord Chamberlain's company, which became the King's Men on the accession of James I in 1603. Shakespeare married Anne Hathaway in 1582, by whom he had two daughters and a son, Hamnet, who died in childhood. Towards the end of his life he loosened his ties with London, and retired to New Place, his substantial property in Stratford that he had bought in 1597. He died on 23rd April 1616 aged 52, and is buried in Holy Trinity Church, Stratford.

Further reading:
L. Lerner and L. Lob, '*Coriolanus:* Brecht and Shakespeare, *Shakespeare Newsletter*, XVII, 1959, p.56

M.W. MacCallum, *Shakespeare's Roman Plays*

J.L. Simmons, *Shakespeare's Pagan World*

Robert Speaight, *Shakespeare on the Stage*, 1973

CORIOLANUS

The scene: Rome and the neighbourhood; Corioli and the neighbourhood; Antium

CHARACTERS IN THE PLAY

CAIUS MARCIUS, *afterwards* CAIUS MARCIUS CORIOLANUS
TITUS LARTIUS,
COMINIUS, } *generals against the Volscians*
MENENIUS AGRIPPA, *friend to Coriolanus*
SICINIUS VELUTUS,
JUNIUS BRUTUS, } *tribunes of the people*
YOUNG MARCIUS, *son to Coriolanus*
A Roman Herald
TULLUS AUFIDIUS, *general of the Volscians*
Lieutenant to Aufidius
Conspirators with Aufidius
A Citizen of Antium
Two Volscian Guards

VOLUMNIA, *mother to Coriolanus*
VIRGILIA, *wife to Coriolanus*
VALERIA, *friend to Virgilia*
Gentlewoman attending on Virgilia
Usher attending on Valeria

Roman and Volscian Senators, Patricians, Ædiles, Lictors, Soldiers, Citizens, Messengers, Servants to Aufidius, and other Attendants.

THE TRAGEDY OF
CORIOLANUS

[1. 1.]   *Rome. A street*

'*Enter a company of mutinous Citizens, with staves,
clubs, and other weapons*'

1 *Citizen*. Before we proceed any further, hear me
speak.

All. Speak, speak.

1 *Citizen*. You are all resolved rather to die than to
famish?

All. Resolved, resolved.

1 *Citizen*. First, you know Caius Marcius is chief
enemy to the people.

All. We know't, we know't.

1 *Citizen*. Let us kill him, and we'll have corn at our 10
own price. Is't a verdict?

All. No more talking on't; let it be done. Away,
away!

2 *Citizen*. One word, good citizens.

1 *Citizen*. We are accounted poor citizens, the
patricians good. What authority surfeits on would
relieve us. If they would yield us but the superfluity
while it were wholesome, we might guess they relieved
us humanely; but they think we are too dear: the lean-
ness that afflicts us, the object of our misery, is as an 20
inventory to particularize their abundance; our sufferance is a gain to them. Let us revenge this with our
pikes ere we become rakes; for the gods know I speak
this in hunger for bread, not in thirst for revenge.

2 *Citizen.* Would you proceed especially against Caius Marcius?

1 *Citizen.* Against him first: he's a very dog to the commonalty.

2 *Citizen.* Consider you what services he has done
30 for his country?

1 *Citizen.* Very well, and could be content to give him good report for't, but that he pays himself with being proud.

2 *Citizen.* Nay, but speak not maliciously.

1 *Citizen.* I say unto you, what he hath done famously he did it to that end; though soft-conscienced men can be content to say it was for his country, he did it partly to please his mother and to be proud, which he is, even to the altitude of his virtue.

40 2 *Citizen.* What he cannot help in his nature you account a vice in him. You must in no way say he is covetous.

1 *Citizen.* If I must not, I need not be barren of accusations; he hath faults (with surplus) to tire in repetition. ['*shouts*']. What shouts are these? The other side o' the city is risen: why stay we prating here? To th' Capitol!

All. Come, come.

1 *Citizen.* Soft! who comes here?

'*Enter MENENIUS AGRIPPA*'

50 2 *Citizen.* Worthy Menenius Agrippa, one that hath always loved the people.

1 *Citizen.* He's one honest enough; would all the rest were so!

Menenius. What work's, my countrymen, in hand?
    Where go you
With bats and clubs? The matter? Speak, I pray you.

1 *Citizen.* Our business is not unknown to th' Senate;
they have had inkling this fortnight what we intend to do,
which now we'll show 'em in deeds. They say poor
suitors have strong breaths: they shall know we have
strong arms too.   60
Menenius. Why, masters, my good friends, mine
    honest neighbours,
Will you undo yourselves?
1 *Citizen.* We cannot, sir; we are undone already.
Menenius. I tell you, friends, most charitable care
Have the patricians of you. For your wants,
Your suffering in this dearth, you may as well
Strike at the heaven with your staves as lift them
Against the Roman state, whose course will on
The way it takes; cracking ten thousand curbs
Of more strong link asunder than can ever   70
Appear in your impediment. For the dearth,
The gods, not the patricians, make it, and
Your knees to them (not arms) must help. Alack,
You are transported by calamity
Thither where more attends you; and you slander
The helms o' th' state, who care for you like fathers,
When you curse them as enemies.
1 *Citizen.* Care for us! True, indeed! They ne'er
cared for us yet. Suffer us to famish, and their store-
houses crammed with grain; make edicts for usury, to 80
support usurers; repeal daily any wholesome act estab-
lished against the rich, and provide more piercing
statutes daily to chain up and restrain the poor. If the
wars eat us not up, they will; and there's all the love
they bear us.
Menenius. Either you must
Confess yourselves wondrous malicious,
Or be accused of folly. I shall tell you

A pretty tale: it may be you have heard it;
90   But, since it serves my purpose, I will venture
To stale't a little more.
   I *Citizen*. Well, I'll hear it, sir: yet you must not
think to fob off our disgrace with a tale: but, an't please
you, deliver.
   Menenius. There was a time when all the
        body's members
Rebelled against the Belly; thus accused it:
That only like a gulf it did remain
I' th' midst o' th' body, idle and unactive,
Still cupboarding the viand, never bearing
100 Like labour with the rest; where th' other instruments
Did see and hear, devise, instruct, walk, feel,
And, mutually participate, did minister
Unto the appetite and affection common
Of the whole body. The Belly answered—
   I *Citizen*. Well, sir, what answer made the Belly?
   Menenius. Sir, I shall tell you. With a kind of smile,
Which ne'er came from the lungs, but even thus—
For, look you, I may make the Belly smile
As well as speak—it tauntingly replied
110 To th' discontented members, the mutinous parts
That envied his receipt; even so most fitly
As you malign our senators for that
They are not such as you.
   I *Citizen*.   Your Belly's answer—What?
The kingly crownéd head, the vigilant eye,
The counsellor heart, the arm our soldier,
Our steed the leg, the tongue our trumpeter,
With other muniments and petty helps
In this our fabric, if that they—
   Menenius.   What then?
'Fore me, this fellow speaks! what then? what then?

1 *Citizen.* Should by the cormorant Belly   120
   be restrained,
Who is the sink o' th' body,—
   Menenius.   Well, what then?
1 *Citizen.* The former agents, if they did complain,
What could the Belly answer?
   Menenius.   I will tell you;
If you'll bestow a small (of what you have little)
Patience awhile, you'st hear the belly's answer.
   1 *Citizen.* You're long about it.
   Menenius.   Note me this, good friend;
Your most grave Belly was deliberate,
Not rash like his accusers, and thus answered:
'True is it, my incorporate friends,' quoth he,
'That I receive the general food at first,   130
Which you do live upon; and fit it is,
Because I am the storehouse and the shop
Of the whole body. But, if you do remember,
I send it through the rivers of your blood,
Even to the court, the heart, to th'seat o' th' brain;
And, through the cranks and offices of man,
The strongest nerves and small inferior veins
From me receive that natural competency
Whereby they live: and though that all at once,
You, my good friends'—this says the Belly, mark me— 140
   1 *Citizen.* Ay, sir; well, well.
   Menenius.   'Though all at once cannot
See what I do deliver out to each,
Yet I can make my audit up, that all
From me do back receive the flour of all,
And leave me but the bran.' What say you to't?
   1 *Citizen.* It was an answer. How apply you this?
   Menenius. The senators of Rome are this good Belly,
And you the mutinous members: for examine

Their counsels and their cares, digest things rightly
150 Touching the weal o'th' common, you shall find
No public benefit which you receive
But it proceeds or comes from them to you,
And no way from yourselves. What do you think,
You, the great toe of this assembly?
   1 *Citizen.* I the great toe! why the great toe?
   Menenius. For that, being one o'th' lowest,
     basest, poorest,
Of this most wise rebellion, thou goest foremost.
Thou rascal, that art worst in blood to run,
Lead'st first to win some vantage.
160 But make you ready your stiff bats and clubs:
Rome and her rats are at the point of battle;
The one side must have bale.

        Enter CAIUS MARCIUS

                  Hail, noble Marcius!
   Marcius. Thanks. What's the matter, you
     dissentious rogues
That, rubbing the poor itch of your opinion,
Make yourselves scabs?
   1 *Citizen.*   We have ever your good word.
   Marcius. He that will give good words to thee
     will flatter
Beneath abhorring. What would you have, you curs,
That like nor peace nor war? the one affrights you,
The other makes you proud. He that trusts to you,
170 Where he should find you lions, finds you hares;
Where foxes, geese: you are no surer, no,
Than is the coal of fire upon the ice,
Or hailstone in the sun. Your virtue is
To make him worthy whose offence subdues him
And curse that justice did it. Who deserves greatness

Deserves your hate. And your affections are
A sick man's appetite, who desires most that
Which would increase his evil. He that depends
Upon your favours swims with fins of lead
And hews down oaks with rushes. Hang ye! Trust ye? 180
With every minute you do change a mind,
And call him noble that was now your hate,
Him vile that was your garland. What's the matter
That in these several places of the city
You cry against the noble Senate, who
(Under the gods) keep you in awe, which else
Would feed on one another? What's their seeking?
   Menenius. For corn at their own rates, whereof
       they say
The city is well stored.
   Marcius.   Hang 'em! They say!
They'll sit by th'fire, and presume to know   190
What's done i'th' Capitol: who's like to rise,
Who thrives and who declines; side factions and
      give out
Conjectural marriages, making parties strong,
And feebling such as stand not in their liking
Below their cobbled shoes. They say there's
      grain enough!
Would the nobility lay aside their ruth,
And let me use my sword, I'd make a quarry
With thousands of these quartered slaves, as high
As I could pick my lance.
   Menenius. Nay, these are all most
      thoroughly persuaded;   200
For though abundantly they lack discretion,
Yet are they passing cowardly. But, I beseech you,
What says the other troop?
   Marcius.   They are dissolved: hang 'em!

They said they were an-hungry; sighed forth proverbs—
That hunger broke stone walls, that dogs must eat,
That meat was made for mouths, that the gods sent not
Corn for the rich men only: with these shreds
They vented their complainings; which being answered,
And a petition granted them—a strange one,
210 To break the heart of generosity
And make bold power look pale—they threw their caps
As they would hang them on the horns o'th' moon,
Shouting their emulation.
   Menenius.   What is granted them?
   Marcius. Five tribunes to defend their vulgar wisdoms,
Of their own choice. One's Junius Brutus, one
Sicinius Velutus, and—I know not. 'Sdeath!
The rabble should have first unroofed the city,
Ere so prevailed with me: it will in time
Win upon power and throw forth greater themes
220 For insurrection's arguing.
   Menenius.   This is strange.
   Marcius. Go, get you home, you fragments!

       '*Enter a Messenger, hastily*'

Messenger. Where's Caius Marcius?
Marcius.   Here: what's the matter?
Messenger. The news is, sir, the Volsces are in arms.
Marcius. I am glad on 't: then we shall ha' means
    to vent
Our musty superfluity. See, our best elders.

Enter COMINIUS, TITUS LARTIUS, *and other Senators;*
    JUNIUS BRUTUS *and* SICINIUS VELUTUS

  1 *Senator.* Marcius, 'tis true that you have lately
    told us;
The Volsces are in arms.

Marcius.   They have a leader,
Tullus Aufidius, that will put you to 't.
I sin in envying his nobility;
And were I anything but what I am,   230
I would wish me only he.
  Cominius.   You have fought together.
  Marcius. Were half to half the world by th' ears,
    and he
Upon my party, I'd revolt, to make
Only my wars with him. He is a lion
That I am proud to hunt.
  1 *Senator.*   Then, worthy Marcius,
Attend upon Cominius to these wars.
  Cominius. It is your former promise.
  Marcius.   Sir, it is,
And I am constant. Titus Lartius, thou
Shalt see me once more strike at Tullus' face.
What, art thou stiff? stand'st out?
  Titus.   No, Caius Marcius; 240
I'll lean upon one crutch and fight with t'other
Ere stay behind this business.
  Menenius.   O, true-bred!
  1 *Senator.* Your company to th' Capitol; where
    I know
Our greatest friends attend us.
  Titus.   [*to Cominius.*] Lead you on.
[*to Marcius.*] Follow Cominius; we must follow you;
Right worthy you priority.
  Cominius.   Noble Marcius!
  1 *Senator.* [*to the citizens*] Hence to your homes;
    be gone!
  Marcius.   Nay, let them follow.
The Volsces have much corn; take these
    rats thither

To gnaw their garners. ['*citizens steal away*';]
    Worshipful mutineers,
250 Your valour puts well forth. Pray, follow.

                    All go but Sicinius and Brutus linger

Sicinius. Was ever man so proud as is this Marcius?
Brutus. He has no equal.
Sicinius. When we were chosen tribunes for
    the people—
Brutus. Marked you his lip and eyes?
Sicinius.   Nay, but his taunts.
Brutus. Being moved, he will not spare to gird
    the gods.
Sicinius. Bemock the modest moon.
Brutus. The present wars devour him! He is grown
Too proud to be so valiant.
Sicinius.   Such a nature,
Tickled with good success, disdains the shadow
260 Which he treads on at noon. But I do wonder
His insolence can brook to be commanded
Under Cominius.
Brutus.   Fame, at the which he aims,
In whom already he's well graced, can not
Better be held, nor more attained, than by
A place below the first: for what miscarries
Shall be the general's fault, though he perform
To th' utmost of a man; and giddy censure
Will then cry out of Marcius 'O, if he
Had borne the business!'
Sicinius.   Besides, if things go well,
270 Opinion, that so sticks on Marcius, shall
Of his demerits rob Cominius.
Brutus.   Come:
Half all Cominius' honours are to Marcius,
Though Marcius earned them not; and all his faults

To Marcius shall be honours, though indeed
In aught he merit not.
 Sicinius.   Let's hence, and hear
How the dispatch is made; and in what fashion,
More than his singularity, he goes
Upon this present action.
 Brutus.   Let's along.   *[they go*

[1. 2.]   *Corioli. The Senate-House*

 '*Enter* TULLUS AUFIDIUS, *with Senators of Corioli*'

 1 *Senator.* So, your opinion is, Aufidius,
That they of Rome are ent'red in our counsels,
And know how we proceed.
 Aufidius.   Is it not yours?
What ever hath been thought on in this state
That could be brought to bodily act ere Rome
Had circumvention? 'Tis not four days gone
Since I heard thence: these are the words: I think
I have the letter here: yes, here it is:
[*reads*] 'They have pressed a power, but it is
  not known
Whether for east or west. The dearth is great; 10
The people mutinous: and it is rumoured,
Cominius, Marcius your old enemy
(Who is of Rome worse hated than of you),
And Titus Lartius, a most valiant Roman,
These three lead on this preparation
Whither 'tis bent: most likely 'tis for you:
Consider of it.'
 1 *Senator.* Our army's in the field:
We never yet made doubt but Rome was ready
To answer us.

Aufidius.   Nor did you think it folly
20 To keep your great pretences veiled till when
They needs must show themselves; which in
        the hatching,
It seemed, appeared to Rome. By the discovery
We shall be short'ned in our aim, which was
To take in many towns ere almost Rome
Should know we were afoot.
    2 Senator.   Noble Aufidius,
Take your commission; hie you to your bands:
Let us alone to guard Corioli.
If they set down before 's, for the remove
Bring up your army; but I think you'll find
30 They've not prepared for us.
    Aufidius.   O, doubt not that;
I speak from certainties. Nay, more,
Some parcels of their power are forth already,
And only hitherward. I leave your honours.
If we and Caius Marcius chance to meet,
'Tis sworn between us we shall ever strike
Till one can do no more.
    All.   The gods assist you!
Aufidius. And keep your honours safe!
    1 Senator.   Farewell.
    2 Senator.   Farewell.
    All. Farewell.   [*they go*

[1. 3.]   *Rome. A room in Marcius' house*

'*Enter* VOLUMNIA *and* VIRGILIA, *mother and wife to
Marcius: they set them down on two low stools, and sew*'

Volumnia. I pray you, daughter, sing, or express
yourself in a more comfortable sort: if my son were my

husband, I should freelier rejoice in that absence wherein he won honour than in the embracements of his bed
where he would show most love. When yet he was but
tender-bodied, and the only son of my womb; when
youth with comeliness plucked all gaze his way; when,
for a day of kings' entreaties, a mother should not sell
him an hour from her beholding; I, considering how
honour would become such a person—that it was no 10
better than picture-like to hang by th'wall, if renown
made it not stir—was pleased to let him seek danger
where he was like to find fame. To a cruel war I sent
him, from whence he returned his brows bound with
oak. I tell thee, daughter, I sprang not more in joy at
first hearing he was a man-child than now in first seeing
he had proved himself a man.

Virgilia. But had he died in the business, madam,
how then?

Volumnia. Then his good report should have been my 20
son; I therein would have found issue. Hear me profess
sincerely: had I a dozen sons, each in my love alike,
and none less dear than thine and my good Marcius,
I had rather had eleven die nobly for their country than
one voluptuously surfeit out of action.

'*Enter a Gentlewoman*'

Gentlewoman. Madam, the Lady Valeria is come to
visit you.

Virgilia. Beseech you give me leave to retire myself.

Volumnia. Indeed, you shall not.
Methinks I hear hither your husband's drum;   30
See him pluck Aufidius down by th' hair;
As children from a bear, the Volsces shunning him.
Methinks I see him stamp thus, and call thus:
'Come on, you cowards! you were got in fear,

Though you were born in Rome.' His bloody brow
With his mailed hand then wiping, forth he goes,
Like to a harvest-man that's tasked to mow
Or all or lose his hire.

    Virgilia. His bloody brow? O Jupiter, no blood!

40 *Volumnia.* Away, you fool! It more becomes a man
Than gilt his trophy. The breasts of Hecuba,
When she did suckle Hector, looked not lovelier
Than Hector's forehead when it spit forth blood
At Grecian sword, contemning. Tell Valeria
We are fit to bid her welcome.   [*Gentlewoman goes*

    Virgilia. Heavens bless my lord from fell Aufidius!

    Volumnia. He'll beat Aufidius' head below his knee,
And tread upon his neck.

Re-enter Gentlewoman with VALERIA and her Usher

    Valeria. My ladies both, good day to you.

50 *Volumnia.* Sweet madam!

    Virgilia. I am glad to see your ladyship.

    Valeria. How do you both? you are manifest house-
keepers. What are you sewing here? A fine spot, in
good faith. How does your little son?

    Virgilia. I thank your ladyship; well, good madam.

    Volumnia. He had rather see the swords and hear a
drum than look upon his schoolmaster.

    Valeria. O' my word, the father's son: I'll swear 'tis
a very pretty boy. O' my troth, I looked upon him

60 o' Wednesday half an hour together: has such a confirmed countenance! I saw him run after a gilded
butterfly; and when he caught it, he let it go again; and
after it again; and over and over he comes, and up
again; catched it again: or whether his fall enraged
him, or how 'twas, he did so set his teeth, and tear it;
O, I warrant, how he mammocked it!

Volumnia. One on's father's moods.

Valeria. Indeed, la, 'tis a noble child.

Virgilia. A crack, madam.

Valeria. Come, lay aside your stitchery; I must have 70
you play the idle huswife with me this afternoon.

Virgilia. No, good madam; I will not out of doors.

Valeria. Not out of doors!

Volumnia. She shall, she shall.

Virgilia. Indeed, no, by your patience; I'll not over
the threshold till my lord return from the wars.

Valeria. Fie, you confine yourself most unreasonably;
come, you must go visit the good lady that lies in.

Virgilia. I will wish her speedy strength, and visit her
with my prayers; but I cannot go thither.　　　80

Volumnia. Why I pray you?

Virgilia. 'Tis not to save labour, nor that I want love.

Valeria. You would be another Penelope; yet, they
say, all the yarn she spun in Ulysses' absence did but fill
Ithaca full of moths. Come; I would your cambric
were sensible as your finger, that you might leave
pricking it for pity. Come, you shall go with us.

Virgilia. No, good madam, pardon me; indeed, I will
not forth.

Valeria. In truth, la, go with me, and I'll tell you 90
excellent news of your husband.

Virgilia. O, good madam, there can be none yet.

Valeria. Verily, I do not jest with you; there came
news from him last night.

Virgilia. Indeed, madam?

Valeria. In earnest, it's true; I heard a senator speak
it. Thus it is: the Volsces have an army forth; against
whom Cominius the general is gone, with one part of
our Roman power: your lord and Titus Lartius are set
down before their city Corioli; they nothing doubt 100

prevailing, and to make it brief wars. This is true, on mine honour; and so, I pray, go with us.

Virgilia. Give me excuse, good madam; I will obey you in every thing hereafter.

Volumnia. Let her alone, lady; as she is now, she will but disease our better mirth.

Valeria. In troth, I think she would. Fare you well, then. Come, good sweet lady. Prithee, Virgilia, turn thy solemness out o' door, and go along with us.

110 *Virgilia.* No, at a word, madam; indeed, I must not. I wish you much mirth.

Valeria. Well then, farewell.   *[they go*

[1. 4.]   *Before the gates of Corioli*

Enter MARCIUS, TITUS LARTIUS, Captains and Soldiers, with drum, trumpet, and colours. To them a Messenger

Marcius. Yonder comes news: a wager they have met.

Lartius. My horse to yours, no.

Marcius.   'Tis done.

Lartius.   Agreed.

Marcius. Say, has our general met the enemy?

Messenger. They lie in view, but have not spoke as yet.

Lartius. So, the good horse is mine.

Marcius.   I'll buy him of you.

Lartius. No, I'll nor sell nor give him: lend you him I will

For half a hundred years. *[to a trumpeter]* Summon the town.

Marcius. How far off lie these armies?

Messenger.   Within this mile and half.

Marcius. Then shall we hear their 'larum, and
　　they ours.
Now, Mars, I prithee, make us quick in work,
That we with smoking swords may march from hence　10
To help our fielded friends! Come, blow thy blast.

> '*They sound a parley. Enter two Senators*
> *with others, on the walls*'

Tullus Aufidius, is he within your walls?
　1 *Senator.* No, nor a man but fears you less than he;
That's lesser than a little. ['*drum afar off*'] Hark, our
　　drums
Are bringing forth our youth. We'll break our walls
Rather than they shall pound us up: our gates,
Which yet seem shut, we have but pinned with rushes;
They'll open of themselves. ['*alarum far off*'] Hark
　　you, far off!
There is Aufidius. List what work he makes
Amongst your cloven army.　　　　　　　　　　　　20
　Marcius.　　　　　　　　O, they are at it!
　Lartius. Their noise be our instruction. Ladders, ho!

> *The gates are flung open and the Volsces make a*
> *sally out upon them*

Marcius. They fear us not, but issue forth
　　their city.
Now put your shields before your hearts, and fight
With hearts more proof than shields. Advance,
　　brave Titus.
They do disdain us much beyond our thoughts,
Which makes me sweat with wrath. Come on,
　　my fellows.
He that retires, I'll take him for a Volsce,
And he shall feel mine edge.

*'Alarum. The Romans are beat back to their trenches.
Enter MARCIUS, cursing'*

30   *Marcius.*   All the contagion of the south light on you,
You shames of Rome! you herd of—Boils and plagues
Plaster you o'er, that you may be abhorred
Farther than seen, and one infect another
Against the wind a mile! You souls of geese
That bear the shapes of men, how have you run
From slaves that apes would beat! Pluto and hell!
All hurt behind! backs red, and faces pale
With flight and agued fear! Mend and charge home,
Or, by the fires of heaven, I'll leave the foe,
40   And make my wars on you. Look to't. Come on;
If you'll stand fast, we'll beat them to their wives,
As they us to our trenches.

*'Another alarum'. The Volsces fly, 'and MARCIUS
follows them to the gates'*

So, now the gates are ope: now prove good seconds:
'Tis for the followers Fortune widens them,
Not for the fliers. Mark me, and do the like.
                                        [*enters the gates*

1 *Soldier.* Fool-hardiness; not I.
2 *Soldier.* Nor I.   [*Marcius is shut in*
1 *Soldier.* See, they have shut him in.
All.   To th' pot, I warrant him.
                                        [*'alarum continues'*

'Enter TITUS LARTIUS'

Lartius. What is become of Marcius?
All.   Slain, sir, doubtless.
1 *Soldier.* Following the fliers at the very heels,
50   With them he enters; who, upon the sudden,

Clapped to their gates. He is himself alone,
To answer all the city.
Lartius.   O noble fellow!
Who sensibly outdares his senseless sword,
And when it bows stand'st up! Thou art lost, Marcius!
A carbuncle entire, as big as thou art,
Were not so rich a jewel. Thou wast a soldier
Even to Cato's wish, not fierce and terrible
Only in strokes; but with thy grim looks and
The thunder-like percussion of thy sounds   60
Thou mad'st thine enemies shake, as if the world
Were feverous and did tremble.

The gates re-open, and 'MARCIUS, bleeding, assaulted
by the enemy' is seen within

1 *Soldier.*   Look, sir.
Lartius.   O, 'tis Marcius!
Let's fetch him off, or make remain alike.
                    ['*they fight, and all enter the city*'

[1. 5.]   '*Certain Romans, with spoils*' come
            running from the city

1 *Roman.* This will I carry to Rome.
2 *Roman.* And I this.
3 *Roman.* A murrain on't! I took this for silver.
            [*sounds of the distant battle still heard*

            Enter MARCIUS and TITUS LARTIUS
                    with a trumpeter

Marcius. See here these movers that do prize
        their honours
At a cracked drachma! Cushions, leaden spoons,
Irons of a doit, doublets that hangmen would
Bury with those that wore them, these base slaves,

Ere yet the fight be done, pack up. Down with them!
And hark, what noise the general makes! To him!
10 There is the man of my soul's hate, Aufidius,
Piercing our Romans: then, valiant Titus, take
Convenient numbers to make good the city;
Whilst I, with those that have the spirit, will haste
To help Cominius.

Lartius.   Worthy sir, thou bleed'st;
Thy exercise hath been too violent
For a second course of fight.

Marcius.   Sir, praise me not;
My work hath yet not warmed me. Fare you well:
The blood I drop is rather physical
Than dangerous to me. To Aufidius thus
20 I will appear, and fight.

Lartius.   Now the fair goddess, Fortune,
Fall deep in love with thee; and her great charms
Misguide thy opposers' swords! Bold gentleman,
Prosperity be thy page!

Marcius.   Thy friend no less
Than those she placeth highest! So farewell.

Lartius. Thou worthiest Marcius!   [*Marcius goes*
Go, sound thy trumpet in the market-place;
Call thither all the officers o'th' town,
Where they shall know our mind. Away!

                               [*they hurry forth*

[1. 6.]   *Near the Roman camp*

'*Enter* COMINIUS, *as it were in retire, with soldiers*'

Cominius. Breathe you, my friends: well fought; we
are come off
Like Romans, neither foolish in our stands

Nor cowardly in retire. Believe me, sirs,
We shall be charged again. Whiles we have struck,
By interims and conveying gusts we have heard
The charges of our friends. The Roman gods,
Lead their successes as we wish our own,
That both our powers, with smiling fronts encount'ring,
May give you thankful sacrifice!

'*Enter a Messenger*'

                         Thy news?
Messenger. The citizens of Corioli have issued,   10
And given to Lartius and to Marcius battle:
I saw our party to their trenches driven,
And then I came away.
   Cominius.   Though thou speak'st truth,
Methinks thou speak'st not well. How long is't since?
   Messenger. Above an hour, my lord.
   Cominius. 'Tis not a mile; briefly we heard
     their drums.
How couldst thou in a mile confound an hour,
And bring thy news so late?
   Messenger.   Spies of the Volsces
Held me in chase, that I was forced to wheel
Three or four miles about; else had I, sir,   20
Half an hour since brought my report.

MARCIUS is seen approaching

   Cominius.   Who's yonder
That does appear as he were flayed? O gods!
He has the stamp of Marcius, and I have
Before-time seen him thus.
   Marcius. [*shouts*]   Come I too late?
   Cominius. The shepherd knows not thunder from
     a tabor

More than I know the sound of Marcius' tongue
From every meaner man.

Marcius. [*at hand*]   Come I too late?

Cominius. Ay, if you come not in the blood of others,
But mantled in your own.

Marcius.   O, let me clip ye
30   In arms as sound as when I wooed; in heart
As merry as when our nuptial day was done,
And tapers burned to bedward!   [*they embrace*

Cominius.   Flower of warriors!—
How is't with Titus Lartius?

Marcius. As with a man busied about decrees:
Condemning some to death and some to exile;
Ransoming him or pitying, threat'ning th' other;
Holding Corioli in the name of Rome,
Even like a fawning greyhound in the leash,
To let him slip at will.

Cominius.   Where is that slave
40   Which told me they had beat you to your trenches?
Where is he? call him hither.

Marcius.   Let him alone;
He did inform the truth. But for our gentlemen,
The common file—a plague! tribunes for them!—
The mouse ne'er shunned the cat as they did budge
From rascals worse than they.

Cominius.   But how prevailed you?

Marcius. Will the time serve to tell? I do not think.
Where is the enemy? Are you lords o' th' field?
If not, why cease you till you are so?

Cominius.   Marcius,
We have at disadvantage fought and did
50   Retire to win our purpose.

Marcius. How lies their battle? know you on which side
They have placed their men of trust?

Cominius.   As I guess, Marcius,
Their bands i' th' vaward are the Antiates,
Of their best trust; o'er them Aufidius,
Their very heart of hope.

  Marcius.   I do beseech you,
By all the battles wherein we have fought,
By th' blood we have shed together, by th' vows
We have made to endure friends, that you directly
Set me against Aufidius and his Antiates;
And that you not delay the present, but,   60
Filling the air with swords advanced and darts,
We prove this very hour.

  Cominius.   Though I could wish
You were conducted to a gentle bath,
And balms applied to you, yet dare I never
Deny your asking: take your choice of those
That best can aid your action.

  Marcius.   Those are they
That most are willing. If any such be here—
As it were sin to doubt—that love this painting
Wherein you see me smeared; if any fear
Lesser his person than an ill report;   70
If any think brave death outweighs bad life,
And that his country's dearer than himself;
Let him alone, or so many so minded,
Wave thus, to express his disposition,
And follow Marcius.
        ['*they all shout, and wave their swords; take*
          him up in their arms, and cast up their caps'
O me, alone! Make you a sword of me?
If these shows be not outward, which of you
But is four Volsces? none of you but is
Able to bear against the great Aufidius
A shield as hard as his. A certain number,   80

Though thanks to all, must I select from all: the rest
Shall bear the business in some other fight,
As cause will be obeyed. Please you to march;
And I shall quickly draw out my command,
Which men are best inclined.
    Cominius.   March on, my fellows:
Make good this ostentation, and you shall
Divide in all with us.   *[they march on*

[1. 7.]   *Before the gates of Corioli*

'*TITUS LARTIUS, having set a guard upon* CORIOLI, *going
with drum and trumpet toward* COMINIUS *and* CAIUS
MARCIUS, *enters with a Lieutenant, other Soldiers, and
a Scout*'

   Lartius. So, let the ports be guarded: keep your duties
As I have set them down. If I do send, dispatch
Those centuries to our aid; the rest will serve
For a short holding. If we lose the field,
We cannot keep the town.
    Lieutenant.   Fear not our care, sir.
   Lartius. Hence, and shut your gates upon 's.
Our guider, come; to th' Roman camp conduct us.
                          [they march on

[1. 8.]   *Near the Roman camp*

'*Alarum as in battle.*' *Enter, from opposite sides,*
MARCIUS *amd* AUFIDIUS

   Marcius. I'll fight with none but thee, for I do
      hate thee
Worse than a promise-breaker.

Aufidius.   We hate alike:
Not Afric owns a serpent I abhor
More than thy fame and envy. Fix thy foot.
  Marcius. Let the first budger die the other's slave,
And the gods doom him after!
  Aufidius.   If I fly, Marcius,
Holloa me like a hare.
  Marcius.   Within these three hours, Tullus,
Alone I fought in your Corioli walls,
And made what work I pleased. 'Tis not my blood
Wherein thou seest me masked. For thy revenge   10
Wrench up thy power to th' highest.
  Aufidius.   Wert thou the Hector
That was the whip of your bragged progeny,
Thou shouldst not scape me here.

>   '*Here they fight, and certain Volsces come in
>   the aid of Aufidius*'

Officious, and not valiant, you have shamed me
In your condemnéd seconds.

>   '*Marcius fights till they be driven*' away '*breathless*'

[1. 9.] '*Flourish. Alarum. A retreat is sounded.
Enter, from one side,* COMINIUS *with the Romans; from
    the other side,* MARCIUS, *with his arm in a scarf*'

  Cominius. If I should tell thee o'er this thy day's work,
Thou't not believe thy deeds: but I'll report it
Where senators shall mingle tears with smiles;
Where great patricians shall attend, and shrug,
I' th' end admire; where ladies shall be frighted,
And, gladly quaked, hear more; where the dull tribunes,
That with the fusty plebeians hate thine honours,
Shall say against their hearts 'We thank the gods

Our Rome hath such a soldier.'
10 Yet cam'st thou to a morsel of this feast,
Having fully dined before.

*'Enter TITUS LARTIUS, with his power,
from the pursuit'*

  Lartius.   O general,
Here is the steed, we the caparison!
Hadst thou beheld—
  Marcius.   Pray now, no more: my mother,
Who has a charter to extol her blood,
When she does praise me grieves me. I have done
As you have done—that's what I can: induced
As you have been—that's for my country:
He that has but effected his good will
Hath overta'en mine act.
  Cominius.   You shall not be
20 The grave of your deserving; Rome must know
The value of her own: 'twere a concealment
Worse than a theft, no less than a traducement,
To hide your doings; and to silence that
Which, to the spire and top of praises vouched,
Would seem but modest: therefore, I beseech you,
In sign of what you are, not to reward
What you have done, before our army hear me.
  Marcius. I have some wounds upon me, and
       they smart
To hear themselves rememb'red.
  Cominius.   Should they not,
30 Well might they fester 'gainst ingratitude,
And tent themselves with death. Of all the horses—
Whereof we have ta'en good, and good store—of all
The treasure in this field achieved and city,
We render you the tenth; to be ta'en forth

Before the common distribution at
Your only choice.
  Marcius.   I thank you, general;
But cannot make my heart consent to take
A bribe to pay my sword: I do refuse it,
And stand upon my common part with those
That have upheld the doing.   40

        ['*A long flourish. They all cry* Marcius!
         Marcius! *cast up their caps and lances:*
         Cominius and Lartius stand bare'

  Marcius. May these same instruments, which
    you profane,
Never sound more! When drums and trumpets shall
I' th' field prove flatterers, let courts and cities be
Made all of false-faced soothing!
When steel grows soft as the parasite's silk,
Let him be made a coverture for th' wars!
No more, I say! For that I have not washed
My nose that bled, or foiled some debile wretch,
Which without note here's many else have done,
You shout me forth   50
In acclamations hyperbolical;
As if I loved my little should be dieted
In praises sauced with lies.
  Cominius.   Too modest are you;
More cruel to your good report than grateful
To us that give you truly. By your patience,
If 'gainst yourself you be incensed, we'll put you
(Like one that means his proper harm) in manacles,
Then reason safely with you. Therefore, be it known,
As to us, to all the world, that Caius Marcius
Wears this war's garland: in token of the which,   60
My noble steed, known to the camp, I give him,
With all his trim belonging; and from this time,

3   PSC

For what he did before Corioli, call him,
With all th' applause and clamour of the host,
CAIUS MARCIUS CORIOLANUS.
Bear th' addition nobly ever!
　　　　　　　　　['*flourish; trumpets sound, and drums.*'
All. Caius Marcius Coriolanus!
Coriolanus. I will go wash;
And when my face is fair, you shall perceive
70 Whether I blush, or no. Howbeit, I thank you:
I mean to stride your steed, and at all times
To undercrest your good addition
To th' fairness of my power.
Cominius. 　　　　　　So, to our tent;
Where, ere we do repose us, we will write
To Rome of our success. You, Titus Lartius,
Must to Corioli back: send us to Rome
The best, with whom we may articulate
For their own good and ours.
Lartius. 　　　　　　　I shall, my lord.
Coriolanus. The gods begin to mock me. I, that now
80 Refused most princely gifts, am bound to beg
Of my lord general.
Cominius. 　　　　Take't; 'tis yours. What is't?
Coriolanus. I sometime lay here in Corioli
And at a poor man's house; he used me kindly.
He cried to me; I saw him prisoner;
But then Aufidius was within my view,
And wrath o'erwhelmed my pity. I request you
To give my poor host freedom.
Cominius. 　　　　　　　O, well begged!
Were he the butcher of my son, he should
Be free as is the wind. Deliver him, Titus.
90 *Lartius.* Marcius, his name?
Coriolanus. 　　　　　　By Jupiter, forgot!

I am weary; yea, my memory is tired.
Have we no wine here?
  Cominius.   Go we to our tent:
The blood upon your visage dries; 'tis time
It should be looked to: come.   [*they go*

[1. 10.]   *The camp of the Volsces*

  '*A flourish. Cornets. Enter* TULLUS AUFIDIUS,
    bloody, with two or three soldiers'

Aufidius. The town is ta'en!
  1 *Soldier.* 'Twill be delivered back on good condition.
  Aufidius. Condition!
I would I were a Roman; for I cannot,
Being a Volsce, be that I am. Condition!
What good condition can a treaty find
I' th' part that is at mercy? Five times, Marcius,
I have fought with thee; so often hast thou beat me;
And wouldst do so, I think, should we encounter
As often as we eat. By th' elements,   10
If e'er again I meet him beard to beard,
He's mine or I am his. Mine emulation
Hath not that honour in't it had; for where
I thought to crush him in an equal force,
True sword to sword, I'll potch at him some way,
Or wrath or craft may get him.
  1 *Soldier.*   He's the devil.
  Aufidius. Bolder, though not so subtle. My
    valour's, poisoned
With only suff'ring stain by him; for him
Shall fly out of itself. Nor sleep nor sanctuary,
Being naked, sick, nor fane nor Capitol,   20

The prayers of priests nor times of sacrifice,
Embarquements all of fury, shall lift up
Their rotten privilege and custom 'gainst
My hate to Marcius. Where I find him, were it
At home, upon my brother's guard, even there,
Against the hospitable canon, would I
Wash my fierce hand in's heart. Go you to th' city;
Learn how 'tis held, and what they are that must
Be hostages for Rome.

1 *Soldier.*   Will not you go?

30 *Aufidius.* I am attended at the cypress grove:
      I pray you—
'Tis south the city mills—bring me word thither
How the world goes, that to the pace of it
I may spur on my journey.

1 *Soldier.*   I shall, sir.   [*they go*

[2. 1.]   *Rome. A public place*

'*Enter* MENENIUS, *with the two Tribunes of the people,* SICINIUS, *and* BRUTUS.'

Menenius. The augurer tells me we shall have news to-night.

Brutus. Good or bad?

Menenius. Not according to the prayer of the people, for they love not Marcius.

Sicinius. Nature teaches beasts to know their friends.

Menenius. Pray you, who does the wolf love?

Sicinius. The lamb.

Menenius. Ay, to devour him, as the hungry plebeians
10 would the noble Marcius.

Brutus. He's a lamb indeed, that baas like a bear.

Menenius. He's a bear indeed, that lives like a lamb. You two are old men: tell me one thing that I shall ask you.

Both. Well, sir.

Menenius. In what enormity is Marcius poor in, that you two have not in abundance?

Brutus. He's poor in no one fault, but stored with all.

Sicinius. Especially in pride.

Brutus. And topping all others in boasting.   20

Menenius. This is strange now. Do you two know how you are censured here in the city—I mean of us o'th' right-hand file? do you?

Both. Why, how are we censured?

Menenius. Because you talk of pride now—will you not be angry?

Both. Well, well, sir, well.

Menenius. Why, 'tis no great matter; for a very little thief of occasion will rob you of a great deal of patience. Give your dispositions the reins, and be angry at your 30 pleasures; at the least, if you take it as a pleasure to you in being so. You blame Marcius for being proud?

Brutus. We do it not alone, sir.

Menenius. I know you can do very little alone; for your helps are many, or else your actions would grow wondrous single: your abilities are too infant-like for doing much alone. You talk of pride. O that you could turn your eyes toward the napes of your necks, and make but an interior survey of your good selves! O that you could!   40

Both. What then, sir?

Menenius. Why, then you should discover a brace of unmeriting, proud, violent, testy magistrates (alias fools) as any in Rome.

Sicinius. Menenius, you are known well enough too.

Menenius. I am known to be a humorous patrician, and one that loves a cup of hot wine with not a drop of allaying Tiber in't; said to be something imperfect in favouring the first complaint, hasty and tinder-like upon
50 too trivial motion; one that converses more with the buttock of the night than with the forehead of the morning. What I think I utter, and spend my malice in my breath. Meeting two such wealsmen as you are— I cannot call you Lycurguses—if the drink you give me touch my palate adversely, I make a crooked face at it. I cannot say your worships have delivered the matter well, when I find the ass in compound with the major part of your syllables; and though I must be content to bear with those that say you are reverend grave men,
60 yet they lie deadly that tell you you have good faces. If you see this in the map of my microcosm, follows it that I am known well enough too? what harm can your bisson conspectuities glean out of this character, if I be known well enough too?

Brutus. Come, sir, come, we know you well enough.

Menenius. You know neither me, yourselves, nor any thing. You are ambitious for poor knaves' caps and legs: you wear out a good wholesome forenoon in hearing a cause between an orange-wife and a faucet-
70 seller, and then rejourn the controversy of three-pence to a second day of audience. When you are hearing a matter between party and party, if you chance to be pinched with the colic, you make faces like mummers, set up the bloody flag against all patience, and, in roaring for a chamber-pot, dismiss the controversy bleeding, the more entangled by your hearing. All the peace you make in their cause is calling both the parties knaves. You are a pair of strange ones.

Brutus. Come, come, you are well understood to be

a perfecter giber for the table than a necessary bencher 80
in the Capitol.

Menenius. Our very priests must become mockers, if
they shall encounter such ridiculous subjects as you are.
When you speak best unto the purpose, it is not worth
the wagging of your beards; and your beards deserve
not so honourable a grave as to stuff a botcher's cushion
or to be entombed in an ass's pack-saddle. Yet you must
be saying Marcius is proud; who, in a cheap estimation,
is worth all your predecessors since Deucalion; though
peradventure some of the best of 'em were hereditary 90
hangmen. God-den to your worships: more of your
conversation would infect my brain, being the herdsmen
of the beastly plebeians. I will be bold to take my leave
of you.   [*Brutus and Sicinius stand 'aside'*

'*Enter VOLUMNIA, VIRGILIA, and VALERIA*'

How now, my as fair as noble ladies—and the moon,
were she earthly, no nobler—whither do you follow
your eyes so fast?

Volumnia. Honourable Menenius, my boy Marcius
approaches; for the love of Juno, let's go.

Menenius. Ha? Marcius coming home!   100

Volumnia. Ay, worthy Menenius; and with most
prosperous approbation.

Menenius. Take my cap, Jupiter, and I thank thee.
Hoo! Marcius coming home!

Virgilia.
Valeria. } Nay, 'tis true.

Volumnia. Look, here's a letter from him: the state
hath another, his wife another; and, I think, there's one
at home for you.

Menenius. I will make my very house reel to-night.
A letter for me?   110

Virgilia. Yes, certain, there's a letter for you; I saw 't.

Menenius. A letter for me! it gives me an estate of seven years' health; in which time I will make a lip at the physician: the most sovereign prescription in Galen is but empiricutic, and, to this preservative, of no better report than a horse-drench. Is he not wounded? he was wont to come home wounded.

Virgilia. O, no, no, no.

Volumnia. O, he is wounded; I thank the gods for't.

120 *Menenius.* So do I too, if it be not too much. Brings a' victory in his pocket, the wounds become him.

Volumnia. On's brows, Menenius. He comes the third time home with the oaken garland.

Menenius. Has he disciplined Aufidius soundly?

Volumnia. Titus Lartius writes they fought together, but Aufidius got off.

Menenius. And 'twas time for him too, I'll warrant him that: an he had stayed by him, I would not have been so fidiused for all the chests in Corioli, and the gold

130 that's in them. Is the Senate possessed of this?

Volumnia. Good ladies, let's go. Yes, yes, yes: the Senate has letters from the General, wherein he gives my son the whole name of the war: he hath in this action outdone his former deeds doubly.

Valeria. In troth, there's wondrous things spoke of him.

Menenius. Wondrous! ay, I warrant you, and not without his true purchasing.

Virgilia. The gods grant them true!

140 *Volumnia.* True! pooh-pooh!

Menenius. True! I'll be sworn they are true. Where is he wounded?—[*observing the tribunes*] God save your good worships! Marcius is coming home: he has more cause to be proud.—Where is he wounded?

Volumnia. I' th' shoulder and i' th' left arm: there will be large cicatrices to show the people, when he shall stand for his place. He received in the repulse of Tarquin seven hurts i' th' body.

Menenius. One i' th' neck, and two i' th' thigh—there's nine that I know.　　　150

Volumnia. He had before this last expedition twenty five wounds upon him.

Menenius. Now it's twenty seven: every gash was an enemy's grave. ['*A shout and flourish*'.] Hark! the trumpets.

Volumnia. These are the ushers of Marcius. Before him he carries noise, and behind him he leaves tears: Death, that dark spirit, in's nervy arm doth lie, Which, being advanced, declines, and then men die.

'*A sennet. Trumpets sound. Enter* COMINIUS *the general and* TITUS LARTIUS; *between them,* CORIOLANUS, *crowned with an oaken garland; with Captains and Soldiers, and a Herald*'

Her. Know, Rome, that all alone Marcius did fight　160
Within Corioli gates, where he hath won,
With fame, a name to Caius Marcius; these
In honour follows Coriolanus.
Welcome to Rome, renownéd Coriolanus! ['*flourish*'
　All. Welcome to Rome, renownéd Coriolanus!
　Coriolanus. No more of this, it does offend my heart;
Pray now, no more.
　Cominius.　　　　Look, sir, your mother!
　Coriolanus.　　　　　　　　O, ['*kneels*'
You have, I know, petitioned all the gods
For my prosperity!
　Volumnia.　　　　Nay, my good soldier, up;
My gentle Marcius, worthy Caius, and　　　170

By deed-achieving honour newly named—
What is it?—Coriolanus must I call thee?—
But, O, thy wife!

   Coriolanus.   My gracious silence, hail!
Wouldst thou have laughed had I come coffined home,
That weep'st to see me triumph? Ah, my dear,
Such eyes the widows in Corioli wear,
And mothers that lack sons.

   Menenius.   Now, the gods crown thee!

   Coriolanus. And live you yet? [*sees Valeria*] O my
     sweet lady, pardon.

   Volumnia. I know not where to turn: O, welcome
     home!
180 And welcome, General: and you're welcome all.

   Menenius. A hundred thousand welcomes.
     I could weep
And I could laugh, I am light and heavy. Welcome!
A curse begnaw the very root on's heart
That is not glad to see thee! You are three
That Rome should dote on: yet, by the faith of men,
We have some old crab-trees here at home that will not
Be grafted to your relish. Yet welcome, warriors:
We call a nettle but a nettle, and
The faults of fools but folly.

   Cominius.   Ever right.
190   *Coriolanus.* Menenius, ever, ever.

   Her. Give way there, and go on.

   Coriolanus. [*to wife and mother*] Your hand,
     and yours!
Ere in our own house I do shade my head,
The good patricians must be visited;
From whom I have received not only greetings,
But with them change of honours.

   Volumnia.   I have lived

To see inherited my very wishes
And the buildings of my fancy: only
There's one thing wanting, which I doubt not but
Our Rome will cast upon thee.

Coriolanus.   Know, good mother,
I had rather be their servant in my way   200
Than sway with them in theirs.

Cominius.   On, to the Capitol!

['*Flourish; cornets. Exeunt in state,* as *before.*'
Brutus and Sicinius come forward

Brutus. All tongues speak of him, and the
     bleared sights
Are spectacled to see him. Your prattling nurse
Into a rapture lets her baby cry
While she chats him: the kitchen malkin pins
Her richest lockram 'bout her reechy neck,
Clamb'ring the walls to eye him: stalls, bulks, windows,
Are smothered up, leads filled and ridges horsed
With variable complexions, all agreeing
In earnestness to see him: seld-shown flamens   210
Do press among the popular throngs, and puff
To win a vulgar station: our veiled dames
Commit the war of white and damask in
Their nicely-guarded cheeks to th' wanton spoil
Of Phœbus' burning kisses: such a pother,
As if that whatsoever god who leads him
Were slily crept into his human powers,
And gave him graceful posture.

Sicinius.   On the sudden,
I warrant him consul.

Brutus.   Then our office may
During his power go sleep.   220

Sicinius. He cannot temp'rately transport his honours

From where he should begin and end, but will
Lose those he hath won.
   Brutus.   In that there's comfort.
   Sicinius.   Doubt not
The commoners, for whom we stand, but they
Upon their ancient malice will forget
With the least cause these his new honours; which
That he will give make I as little question
As he is proud to do't.
   Brutus.   I heard him swear,
Were he to stand for consul, never would he
230 Appear i' th' market-place, nor on him put
The napless vesture of humility;
Nor, showing, as the manner is, his wounds
To th' people, beg their stinking breaths.
   Sicinus.   'Tis right.
   Brutus. It was his word. O, he would miss it rather
Than carry it but by the suit of the gentry to him
And the desire of the nobles.
   Sicinius.   I wish no better
Than have him hold that purpose and to put it
In execution.
   Brutus.   'Tis most like he will.
   Sicinius. It shall be to him then as our good wills:
240 A sure destruction.
   Brutus.   So it must fall out
To him or our authorities. For an end,
We must suggest the people in what hatred
He still hath held them; that to's power he would
Have made them mules, silenced their pleaders and
Dispropertied their freedoms; holding them,
In human action and capacity,
Of no more soul nor fitness for the world
Than camels in the war, who have their provand

Only for bearing burthens, and sore blows
For sinking under them.
  Sicinius.   This, as you say, suggested   250
At some time when his soaring insolence
Shall touch the people—which time shall not want,
If he be put upon't, and that's as easy
As to set dogs on sheep—will be the fire
To kindle their dry stubble; and their blaze
Shall darken him for ever.

'*Enter a Messenger*'

  Brutus.   What's the matter?
  Messenger. You are sent for to the Capitol.
    'Tis thought
That Marcius shall be consul.
I have seen the dumb men throng to see him and
The blind to hear him speak; matrons flung gloves,   260
Ladies and maids their scarfs and handkerchers,
Upon him as he passed; the nobles bended,
As to Jove's statue, and the commons made
A shower and thunder with their caps and shouts.
I never saw the like.
  Brutus.   Let's to the Capitol,
And carry with us ears and eyes for th' time,
But hearts for the event.
  Sicinius.   Have with you.   [*they go*

[2. 2.] *Rome. The Senate House at the Capitol*

'*Enter two Officers, to lay cushions*'

1 *Officer.* Come, come, they are almost here. How many stand for consulships?

2 *Officer.* Three, they say: but 'tis thought of every one Coriolanus will carry it.

1 *Officer.* That's a brave fellow; but he's vengeance proud, and loves not the common people.

2 *Officer.* Faith, there hath been many great men that have flattered the people, who ne'er loved them; and there be many that they have loved, they know not
10 wherefore: so that, if they love they know not why, they hate upon no better a ground. Therefore, for Coriolanus neither to care whether they love or hate him manifests the true knowledge he has in their disposition; and out of his noble carelessness lets them plainly see't.

1 *Officer.* If he did not care whether he had their love or no, he waved indifferently 'twixt doing them neither good nor harm. But he seeks their hate with greater devotion than they can render it him, and leaves nothing undone that may fully discover him their opposite.
20 Now, to seem to affect the malice and displeasure of the people is as bad as that which he dislikes, to flatter them for their love.

2 *Officer.* He hath deserved worthily of his country; and his ascent is not by such easy degrees as those who, having been supple and courteous to the people, bonneted, without any further deed to have them at all, into their estimation and report. But he hath so planted his honours in their eyes and his actions in their hearts that for their tongues to be silent and not confess so
30 much were a kind of ingrateful injury; to report other-

wise were a malice that, giving itself the lie, would pluck
reproof and rebuke from every ear that heard it.

1 *Officer*. No more of him; he's a worthy man. Make
way, they are coming.

'*A sennet. Enter the Patricians and the Tribunes of the
People, Lictors before them;* CORIOLANUS, MENENIUS,
COMINIUS *the Consul.* SICINIUS *and* BRUTUS *take their
places by themselves*'

Menenius. Having determined of the Volsces, and
To send for Titus Lartius, it remains,
As the main point of this our after-meeting,
To gratify his noble service that
Hath thus stood for his country: therefore, please you
Most reverend and grave elders, to desire   40
The present consul, and last general
In our well-found successes, to report
A little of that worthy work performed
By Caius Marcius Coriolanus; whom
We met here both to thank and to remember
With honours like himself.

1 *Senator.*   Speak, good Cominius:
Leave nothing out for length, and make us think
Rather our state's defective for requital
Than we to stretch it out. [*to the Tribunes*] Masters
     o' th' people,
We do request your kindest ears; and, after,   50
Your loving motion toward the common body,
To yield what passes here.

Sicinius.   We are convented
Upon a pleasing treaty, and have hearts
Inclinable to honour and advance
The theme of our assembly.

Brutus.   Which the rather

We shall be blessed to do, if he remember
A kinder value of the people than
He hath hereto prized them at.

Menenius.   That's off, that's off;
I would you rather had been silent. Please you
60 To hear Cominius speak?

Brutus.   Most willingly:
But yet my caution was more pertinent
Than the rebuke you give it.

Menenius.   He loves your people;
But tie him not to be their bedfellow.
Worthy Cominius, speak.

     ['*Coriolanus rises and offers to go away*']
            Nay, keep your place.

1 *Senator.* Sit, Coriolanus; never shame to hear
What you have nobly done.

Coriolanus.   Your honours' pardon:
I had rather have my wounds to heal again
Than hear say how I got them.

Brutus.   Sir, I hope
My words disbenched you not.

Coriolanus.   No, sir: yet oft,
70 When blows have made me stay, I fled from words.
You soothed not, therefore hurt not: but your people,
I love them as they weigh—

Menenius.   Pray now, sit down.

Coriolanus. I had rather have one scratch my head
    i' th' sun
When the alarum were struck than idly sit
To hear my nothings monstered.   [*he goes*

Menenius.   Masters of the people,
Your multiplying spawn how can he flatter—
That's thousand to one good one—when you
    now see

He had rather venture all his limbs for honour
Than one on's ears to hear it? Proceed, Cominius.
  Cominius. I shall lack voice: the deeds of Coriolanus 80
Should not be uttered feebly. It is held
That valour is the chiefest virtue and
Most dignifies the haver: if it be,
The man I speak of cannot in the world
Be singly counterpoised. At sixteen years,
When Tarquin made a head for Rome, he fought
Beyond the mark of others: our then dictator,
Whom with all praise I point at, saw him fight,
When with his Amazonian chin he drove
The bristled lips before him: he bestrid   90
An o'erpressed Roman, and i' th' consul's view
Slew three opposers: Tarquin's self he met,
And struck him on his knee: in that day's feats,
When he might act the woman in the scene,
He proved best man i' th' field, and for his meed
Was brow-bound with the oak. His pupil age
Man-ent'red thus, he waxéd like a sea;
And, in the brunt of seventeen battles since,
He lurched all swords of the garland. For this last,
Before and in Corioli, let me say,   100
I cannot speak him home. He stopped the fliers,
And by his rare example made the coward
Turn terror into sport: as weeds before
A vessel under sail, so men obeyed,
And fell below his stem. His sword, death's stamp,
Where it did mark, it took; from face to foot
He was a thing of blood, whose every motion
Was timed with dying cries. Alone he ent'red
The mortal gate of th' city, which he painted
With shunless destiny; aidless came off,   110
And with a sudden re-enforcement struck

Corioli like a planet. Now all's his,
When by and by the din of war 'gan pierce
His ready sense, then straight his doubled spirit
Re-quickened what in flesh was fatigate,
And to the battle came he; where he did
Run reeking o'er the lives of men, as if
'Twere a perpetual spoil: and till we called
Both field and city ours, he never stood
120 To ease his breast with panting.

Menenius.   Worthy man!

1 *Senator.* He cannot but with measure fit
    the honours
Which we devise him.

Cominius.   Our spoils he kicked at,
And looked upon things precious as they were
The common muck of the world: he covets less
Than misery itself would give, rewards
His deeds with doing them, and is content
To spend the time to end it.

Menenius.   He's right noble:
Let him be called for.

1 *Senator.*   Call Coriolanus.

Officer. He doth appear.

CORIOLANUS *returns*

130 *Menenius.* The Senate, Coriolanus, are well pleased
To make thee consul.

Coriolanus.   I do owe them still
My life and services.

Menenius.   It then remains
That you do speak to the people.

Coriolanus.   I do beseech you
Let me o'erleap that custom, for I cannot
Put on the gown, stand naked, and entreat them,

For my wounds' sake, to give their suffrage: please you
That I may pass this doing.

Sicinius.   Sir, the people
Must have their voices; neither will they bate
One jot of ceremony.

Menenius.   Put them not to't.
Pray you, go fit you to the custom, and   140
Take to you, as your predecessors have,
Your honour with your form.

Coriolanus.   It is a part
That I shall blush in acting, and might well
Be taken from the people.

(*Brutus.*   Mark you that.
Coriolanus. To brag unto them, 'Thus I did, and thus!'
Show them th' unaching scars which I should hide,
As if I had received them for the hire
Of their breath only!

(*Menenius.* Do not stand upon't.
[*aloud*] We recommend to you, tribunes of the people,
Our purpose to them: and to our noble consul   150
Wish we all joy and honour.

Senators. To Coriolanus come all joy and honour!

                    [*Flourish of cornets; all leave the Senate
                              House but Sicinius and Brutus*

Brutus. You see how he intends to use the people.
Sicinius. May they perceive's intent! He will
     require them,
As if he did contemn what he requested
Should be in them to give.

Brutus.   Come, we'll inform them
Of our proceedings here. On th' market-place,
I know, they do attend us.   [*they follow*

'Enter seven or eight Citizens'

1 *Citizen*. Once, if he do require our voices, we ought not to deny him.

2 *Citizen*. We may, sir, if we will.

3 *Citizen*. We have power in ourselves to do it, but it is a power that we have no power to do: for if he show us his wounds and tell us his deeds, we are to put our tongues into those wounds and speak for them; so, if he tell us his noble deeds, we must also tell him our noble acceptance of them. Ingratitude is monstrous: and for 10 the multitude to be ingrateful, were to make a monster of the multitude; of the which we being members, should bring ourselves to be monstrous members.

1 *Citizen*. And to make us no better thought of, a little help will serve; for once we stood up about the corn, he himself stuck not to call us the many-headed multitude.

3 *Citizen*. We have been called so of many; not that our heads are some brown, some black, some abram, some bald, but that our wits are so diversely coloured: 20 and truly I think, if all our wits were to issue out of one skull, they would fly east, west, north, south, and their consent of one direct way should be at once to all the points o' th' compass.

2 *Citizen*. Think you so? Which way do you judge my wit would fly?

3 *Citizen*. Nay, your wit will not so soon out as another man's will; 'tis strongly wedged up in a block-head; but if it were at liberty, 'twould, sure, southward.

2 *Citizen*. Why that way?

30 3 *Citizen*. To lose itself in a fog; where being three

parts melted away with rotten dews, the fourth would
return for conscience sake, to help to get thee a wife.

2 *Citizen.* You are never without your tricks: you
may, you may.

3 *Citizen.* Are you all resolved to give your voices?
But that's no matter, the greater part carries it. I say,
if he would incline to the people, there was never a
worthier man.

'*Enter* CORIOLANUS *in a gown of humility,
with* MENENIUS'

Here he comes, and in the gown of humility: mark his
behaviour. We are not to stay all together, but to come 40
by him where he stands, by ones, by twos, and by
threes. He's to make his requests by particulars; wherein
every one of us has a single honour, in giving him our
own voices with our own tongues: therefore follow me,
and I'll direct you how you shall go by him.

All. Content, content.   [*they go off*

Menenius. O sir, you are not right: have you
          not known
The worthiest men have done 't?

Coriolanus.   What must I say?—
'I pray, sir,'—Plague upon't! I cannot bring
My tongue to such a pace. 'Look, sir, my wounds!   50
I got them in my country's service, when
Some certain of your brethren roared and ran
From th' noise of our own drums.'

Menenius.   O me, the gods!
You must not speak of that: you must desire them
To think upon you.

Coriolanus.   Think upon me! hang 'em!
I would they would forget me, like the virtues
Which our divines lose by 'em.

Menenius.   You'll mar all.
I'll leave you. Pray you, speak to 'em, I pray you,
In wholesome manner.   *[he goes*

Re-enter Second and Third Citizens

Coriolanus.   Bid them wash their faces,
60 And keep their teeth clean. So, here comes a brace.
You know the cause, sir, of my standing here.

3 *Citizen.* We do, sir; tell us what hath brought
you to't.

Coriolanus. Mine own desert.

2 *Citizen.* Your own desert?

Coriolanus. Ay, but not mine own desire.

3 *Citizen.* How not your own desire?

Coriolanus. No, sir, 'twas never my desire yet to
trouble the poor with begging.

70 3 *Citizen.* You must think, if we give you any thing,
we hope to gain by you.

Coriolanus. Well then, I pray, your price o' th'
consulship?

3 *Citizen.* The price is, to ask it kindly.

Coriolanus. Kindly, sir, I pray let me ha't: I have
wounds to show you, which shall be yours in private.
[*to the Second Citizen*] Your good voice, sir; what say
you?

2 *Citizen.* You shall ha' it, worthy sir.

80 *Coriolanus.* A match, sir. There's in all two worthy
voices begged. I have your alms: adieu.

                                [turns from them

3 *Citizen.* But this is something odd.

2 *Citizen.* An 'twere to give again—but 'tis no matter.

                                    [they go
'*Enter two other Citizens*'

Coriolanus. Pray you now, if it may stand with the

tune of your voices that I may be consul, I have here
the customary gown.

4 Citizen. You have deserved nobly of your country,
and you have not deserved nobly.

Coriolanus. Your enigma?

4 Citizen. You have been a scourge to her enemies, 90
you have been a rod to her friends. You have not indeed
loved the common people.

Coriolanus. You should account me the more virtuous,
that I have not been common in my love. I will, sir,
flatter my sworn brother, the people, to earn a dearer
estimation of them; 'tis a condition they account gentle:
and since the wisdom of their choice is rather to have
my hat than my heart, I will practise the insinuating
nod, and be off to them most counterfeitly; that is, sir,
I will counterfeit the bewitchment of some popular 100
man, and give it bountiful to the desirers. Therefore,
beseech you I may be consul.

5 Citizen. We hope to find you our friend; and therefore give you our voices heartily.

4 Citizen. You have received many wounds for your
country.

Coriolanus. I will not seal your knowledge with
showing them. I will make much of your voices and
so trouble you no farther.

Both Citizens. The gods give you joy, sir, heartily! 110
　　　　　　　　　　　　　　　　　　　　　[they go

　Coriolanus. Most sweet voices!
Better it is to die, better to starve,
Than crave the hire which first we do deserve.
Why in this woolvish toge should I stand here,
To beg of Hob and Dick that do appear
Their needless vouches? Custom calls me to't.
What custom wills, in all things should we do't,

The dust on antique time would lie unswept,
And mountainous error be too highly heaped
120 For truth to o'erpeer. Rather than fool it so,
Let the high office and the honour go
To one that would do thus. I am half through:
The one part suffered, the other will I do.

'Enter three Citizens more'

Here come moe voices.
Your voices! For your voices I have fought;
Watched for your voices; for your voices bear
Of wounds two dozen odd; battles thrice six
I have seen, and heard of; for your voices have
Done many things, some less, some more. Your voices!
130 Indeed, I would be consul.

5 Citizen. He has done nobly, and cannot go without
any honest man's voice.

6 Citizen. Therefore let him be consul: the gods give
him joy, and make him good friend to the people!

All. Amen, amen. God save thee, noble consul!

[*they go*

Coriolanus. Worthy voices!

'Enter MENENIUS, with BRUTUS and SICINIUS'

Menenius. You have stood your limitation; and
      the tribunes
Endue you with the people's voice. Remains
That in th' official marks invested you
140 Anon do meet the Senate.

Coriolanus.   Is this done?

Sicinius. The custom of request you have discharged:
The people do admit you, and are summoned.
To meet anon upon your approbation.

Coriolanus. Where? at the Senate House?

Sicinius. There, Coriolanus.

Coriolanus. May I change these garments?

Sicinius. You may, sir.

Coriolanus. That I'll straight do, and, knowing myself again,

Repair to the Senate House.

Menenius. I'll keep you company. Will you along?

Brutus. We stay here for the people.

Sicinius. Fare you well.

　　　[Coriolanus and Menenius depart

He has it now; and, by his looks, methinks　　150

'Tis warm at's heart.

Brutus. With a proud heart he wore

His humble weeds. Will you dismiss the people?

Citizens return

Sicinius. How now, my masters! have you chose this man?

1 Citizen. He has our voices, sir.

Brutus. We pray the gods he may deserve your loves.

2 Citizen. Amen, sir: to my poor unworthy notice,

He mocked us when he begged our voices.

3 Citizen. Certainly;

He flouted us downright.

1 Citizen. No, 'tis his kind of speech—he did not mock us.

2 Citizen. Not one amongst us, save yourself, but says　160

He used us scornfully: he should have showed us

His marks of merit, wounds received for's country.

Sicinius. Why, so he did, I am sure.

All. No, no; no man saw 'em.

3 Citizen. He said he had wounds which he could show in private;

And with his hat, thus waving it in scorn,

'I would be consul,' says he: 'agéd custom,
But by your voices, will not so permit me;
Your voices therefore.' When we granted that,
170 Here was 'I thank you for your voices. Thank you,
Your most sweet voices. Now you have left your voices,
I have no further with you.' Was not this mockery?
   Sicinius. Why either were you ignorant to see't,
Or, seeing it, of such childish friendliness
To yield your voices?
   Brutus.   Could you not have told him—
As you were lessoned—when he had no power,
But was a petty servant to the state,
He was your enemy, ever spake against
Your liberties and the charters that you bear
180 I' th' body of the weal: and now, arriving
A place of potency and sway o' th' state,
If he should still malignantly remain
Fast foe to th' plebeii, your voices might
Be curses to yourselves? You should have said
That as his worthy deeds did claim no less
Than what he stood for, so his gracious nature
Would think upon you for your voices, and
Translate his malice towards you into love,
Standing your friendly lord.
   Sicinius.   Thus to have said,
190 As you were fore-advised, had touched his spirit
And tried his inclination; from him plucked
Either his gracious promise, which you might,
As cause had called you up, have held him to;
Or else it would have galled his surly nature,
Which easily endures not article
Tying him to aught: so, putting him to rage,
You should have ta'en th' advantage of his choler,
And passed him unelected.

Brutus.   Did you perceive
He did solicit you in free contempt
When he did need your loves; and do you think   200
That his contempt shall not be bruising to you
When he hath power to crush? Why, had your bodies
No heart among you? or had you tongues to cry
Against the rectorship of judgement?
Sicinius.   Have you
Ere now denied the asker, and now again,
Of him that did not ask but mock, bestow
Your sued-for tongues?
  3 Citizen. He's not confirmed; we may deny him yet.
  2 Citizen. And will deny him:
I'll have five hundred voices of that sound.   210
  1 Citizen. I twice five hundred, and their friends to
        piece 'em.
  Brutus. Get you hence instantly, and tell
        those friends
They have chose a consul that will from them take
Their liberties, make them of no more voice
Than dogs that are as often beat for barking
As therefore kept to do so.
  Sicinius.   Let them assemble;
And, on a safer judgement, all revoke
Your ignorant election. Enforce his pride
And his old hate unto you: besides, forget not
With what contempt he wore the humble weed,   220
How in his suit he scorned you: but your loves,
Thinking upon his services, took from you
Th' apprehension of his present portance,
Which, gibingly, ungravely, he did fashion
After the inveterate hate he bears you.
  Brutus.   Lay
A fault on us, your tribunes, that we laboured,

No impediment between, but that you must
Cast your election on him.
   Sicinius.   Say you chose him
More after our commandment than as guided
230 By your own true affections; and that your minds,
Pre-occupied with what you rather must do
Than what you should, made you against the grain
To voice him consul. Lay the fault on us.
   Brutus. Ay, spare us not. Say we read lectures to you,
How youngly he began to serve his country,
How long continued; and what stock he springs of,
The noble house o' th' Marcians, from whence came
That Ancus Marcius, Numa's daughter's son,
Who after great Hostilius here was king;
240 Of the same house Publius and Quintus were,
That our best water brought by conduits hither;
[And Censorinus that was so surnamed]
And nobly naméd so, twice being censor,
Was his great ancestor.
   Sicinius.   One thus descended,
That hath beside well in his person wrought
To be set high in place, we did commend
To your remembrances: but you have found,
Scaling his present bearing with his past,
That he's your fixéd enemy, and revoke
250 Your sudden approbation.
   Brutus.   Say you ne'er had done't—
Harp on that still—but by our putting on:
And presently, when you have drawn your number,
Repair to th' Capitol.
   Citizens.   We will so: almost all
Repent in their election.   *[they go*
   Brutus.   Let them go on;
This mutiny were better put in hazard

Than stay, past doubt, for greater:
If, as his nature is, he fall in rage
With their refusal, both observe and answer
The vantage of his anger.
  Sicinius.   To th' Capitol, come:
We will be there before the stream o' th' people;   260
And this shall seem, as partly 'tis, their own,
Which we have goaded onward.   *[they go*

[3. 1.]   *Rome. A street*

'*Cornets. Enter* CORIOLANUS, MENENIUS, *all the Gentry,*
COMINIUS, TITUS LARTIUS, *and other Senators*'

  Coriolanus. Tullus Aufidius then had made new head?
  Lartius. He had, my lord; and that it was
    which caused
Our swifter composition.
  Coriolanus. So then the Volsces stand but as at first;
Ready, when time shall prompt them, to make road
Upon's again.
  Cominius. They are worn, Lord Consul, so
That we shall hardly in our ages see
Their banners wave again.
  Coriolanus.   Saw you Aufidius?
  Lartius. On safeguard he came to me; and did curse
Against the Volsces, for they had so vilely   10
Yielded the town: he is retired to Antium.
  Coriolanus. Spoke he of me?
  Lartius.   He did, my lord.
  Coriolanus.   How? what?
  Lartius. How often he had met you, sword to sword;
That of all things upon the earth he hated

Your person most; that he would pawn his fortunes
To hopeless restitution, so he might
Be called your vanquisher.

   Coriolanus.   At Antium lives he?

   Lartius. At Antium.

   Coriolanus. I wish I had a cause to seek him there,
20 To oppose his hatred fully. Welcome home.

        'Enter SICINIUS and BRUTUS'

Behold, these are the tribunes of the people,
The tongues o' th' common mouth. I do despise them;
For they do prank them in authority,
Against all noble sufferance.

   Sicinius.   Pass no further.

   Coriolanus. Ha? what is that?

   Brutus. It will be dangerous to go on—no further.

   Coriolanus. What makes this change?

   Menenius. The matter?

   Cominius. Hath he not passed the noble and
     the common?

30   *Brutus.* Cominius, no.

   Coriolanus.   Have I had children's voices?

   1 *Senator.* Tribunes, give way; he shall to th'
     market-place.

   Brutus. The people are incensed against him.

   Sicinius.   Stop.
Or all will fall in broil.

   Coriolanus.   Are these your herd?
Must these have voices, that can yield them now,
And straight disclaim their tongues? What are
     your offices?
You being their mouths, why rule you not their teeth?
Have you not set them on?

   Menenius.   Be calm, be calm.

Coriolanus. It is a purposed thing, and grows by plot,
To curb the will of the nobility:
Suffer't, and live with such as cannot rule,   40
Nor ever will be ruled.

Brutus.   Call't not a plot:
The people cry you mocked them; and of late,
When corn was given them gratis, you repined,
Scandaled the suppliants for the people, called them
Time-pleasers, flatterers, foes to nobleness.

Coriolanus. Why, this was known before.

Brutus.   Not to them all.

Coriolanus. Have you informed them sithence?

Brutus.   How! I inform them!

Coriolanus. You are like to do such business.

Brutus.   Not unlike
Each way to better yours.

Coriolanus. Why then should I be consul? By   50
    yond clouds,
Let me deserve so ill as you, and make me
Your fellow tribune.

Sicinius.   You show too much of that
For which the people stir: if you will pass
To where you are bound, you must inquire your way,
Which you are out of, with a gentler spirit,
Or never be so noble as a consul,
Nor yoke with him for tribune.

Menenius.   Let's be calm.

Cominius. The people are abused; set on.
    This palt'ring
Becomes not Rome; nor has Coriolanus
Deserved this so dishonoured rub, laid falsely   60
I' th' plain way of his merit.

Coriolanus.   Tell me of corn!
This was my speech, and I will speak't again—

Menenius. Not now, not now.

1 *Senator.*　　　　　　　Not in this heat, sir, now.

Coriolanus. Now, as I live, I will.

My nobler friends, I crave their pardons. For

The mutable, rank-scented meiny, let them

Regard me as I do not flatter, and

Therein behold themselves. I say again,

In soothing them, we nourish 'gainst our Senate

70 The cockle of rebellion, insolence, sedition,

Which we ourselves have ploughed for, sowed,

　　　and scattered,

By mingling them with us, the honoured number;

Who lack not virtue, no, nor power, but that

Which they have given to beggars.

Menenius.　　　　　　　　Well, no more.

1 *Senator.* No more words, we beseech you.

Coriolanus.　　　　　　　How! no more!

As for my country I have shed my blood,

Not fearing outward force, so shall my lungs

Coin words till their decay against those measles,

Which we disdain should tetter us, yet sought

80 The very way to catch them.

Brutus.　　　　　　You speak o' th' people,

As if you were a god, to punish; not

A man of their infirmity.

Sicinius.　　　　　　'Twere well

We let the people know't.

Menenius.　　　　What, what? his choler?

Coriolanus. Choler!

Were I as patient as the midnight sleep,

By Jove, 'twould be my mind!

Sicinius.　　　　　　It is a mind

That shall remain a poison where it is,

Not poison any further.

Coriolanus.   Shall remain!
Hear you this Triton of the minnows? mark you
His absolute 'shall'?
    Cominius.   'Twas from the canon.
    Coriolanus.   'Shall'!   90
O good but most unwise patricians! Why,
You grave but reckless senators, have you thus
Given Hydra here to choose an officer,
That with his peremptory 'shall,' being but
The horn and noise o' th' monster's, wants not spirit
To say he'll turn your current in a ditch,
And make your channel his? If he have power,
Then vail your ignorance; if none, awake
Your dangerous lenity. If you are learned,
Be not as common fools; if you are not,   100
Let them have cushions by you. You are plebeians,
If they be senators; and they no less,
When, both your voices blended, the great'st taste
Most palates theirs. They choose their magistrate;
And such a one as he, who puts his 'shall,'
His popular 'shall', against a graver bench
Than ever frowned in Greece. By Jove himself,
It makes the consuls base! and my soul aches
To know, when two authorities are up,
Neither supreme, how soon confusion   110
May enter 'twixt the gap of both and take
The one by th' other.
    Cominius.   Well, on to th' market-place.
    Coriolanus. Whoever gave that counsel to give forth
The corn o' th' storehouse gratis, as 'twas used
Sometime in Greece—
    Menenius.   Well, well, no more of that.
    Coriolanus. Though there the people had more
        absolute power,

I say they nourished disobedience, fed
The ruin of the state.
    Brutus.   Why shall the people give
One that speaks thus their voice?
    Coriolanus.   I'll give my reasons,
120 More worthier than their voices. They know the corn
Was not our recompense, resting well assured
They ne'er did service for't. Being pressed to th' war,
Even when the navel of the state was touched,
They would not thread the gates; this kind of service
Did not deserve corn gratis. Being i' th' war,
Their mutinies and revolts, wherein they showed
Most valour, spoke not for them. Th' accusation
Which they have often made against the Senate,
All cause unborn, could never be the native
130 Of our so frank donation. Well, what then?
How shall this bosom multiplied digest
The Senate's courtesy? Let deeds express
What's like to be their words: 'We did request it;
We are the greater poll, and in true fear
They gave us our demands.' Thus we debase
The nature of our seats, and make the rabble
Call our cares fears; which will in time
Break ope the locks o' th' Senate and bring in
The crows to peck the eagles.
    Menenius.   Come, enough.
140 *Brutus.* Enough, with over measure.
    Coriolanus.   No, take more.
What may be sworn by, both divine and human,
Seal what I end withal! This double worship,
Where one part does disdain with cause, the other
Insult without all reason; where gentry, title, wisdom,
Cannot conclude but by the yea and no
Of general ignorance—it must omit

Real necessities, and give way the while
To unstable slightness. Purpose so barred, it follows
Nothing is done to purpose. Therefore, beseech you—
You that will be less fearful than discreet;　　　　150
That love the fundamental part of state
More than you doubt the change on 't; that prefer
A noble life before a long, and wish
To jump a body with a dangerous physic
That's sure of death without it—at once pluck out
The multitudinous tongue; let them not lick
The sweet which is their poison. Your dishonour
Mangles true judgement, and bereaves the state
Of that integrity which should become't;
Not having the power to do the good it would,　　　　160
For th' ill which doth control 't.
　　Brutus.　　　　　　　　　　Has said enough.
　　Sicinius. Has spoken like a traitor and shall answer
As traitors do.
　　Coriolanus. Thou wretch, despite o'erwhelm thee!
What should the people do with these bald tribunes,
On whom depending, their obedience fails
To th' greater bench? In a rebellion,
When what's not meet, but what must be, was law,
Then were they chosen: in a better hour
Let what is meet be said it must be meet,
And throw their power i' th' dust.　　　　170
　　Brutus. Manifest treason!
　　Sicinius.　　　　　　　This a consul? No.
　　Brutus. The ædiles, ho!

　　　　　　　　'*Enter an Ædile*'

　　　　　　　　Let him be apprehended.
　　Sicinius. Go, call the people: [*Ædile goes*] in whose
　　name myself

Attach thee as a traitorous innovator,
A foe to th' public weal. Obey, I charge thee,
And follow to thine answer.

Coriolanus.   Hence, old goat!

Senators, &c. We'll surety him.

Cominius.   Agéd sir, hands off.

Coriolanus. Hence, rotten thing! or I shall shake
thy bones
Out of thy garments.

Sicinius.   Help, ye citizens!

'*Enter a rabble of Plebeians, with the Ædiles*'

180   *Menenius.* On both sides more respect.

Sicinius. Here's he that would take from you all
your power.

Brutus. Seize him, ædiles!

Citizens. Down with him! down with him!

2 Senator. Weapons, weapons, weapons!

                        ['*they all bustle about Coriolanus*'
Cries. 'Tribunes!' 'Patricians!' 'Citizens!' 'What, ho!'
'Sicinius!' 'Brutus!' 'Coriolanus!' 'Citizens!'
'Peace, peace, peace!' 'Stay! hold! peace!'

  Menenius. What is about to be? I am out of breath.
Confusion's near. I cannot speak. You, tribunes
190 To th' people! Coriolanus, patience!
Speak, good Sicinius.

Sicinius.   Hear me, people; peace!

Citizens. Let's hear our tribune: peace!—Speak,
speak, speak.

Sicinius. You are at point to lose your liberties:
Marcius would have all from you; Marcius,
Whom late you have named for consul.

Menenius.   Fie, fie, fie!
This is the way to kindle, not to quench.

1 *Senator.* To unbuild the city, and to lay all flat.

Sicinius. What is the city but the people?

Citizens.   True,
The people are the city.

Brutus. By the consent of all, we were established   200
The people's magistrates.

Citizens.   You so remain.

Menenius. And so are like to do.

Cominius. That is the way to lay the city flat,
To bring the roof to the foundation,
And bury all which yet distinctly ranges,
In heaps and piles of ruin.

Sicinius.   This deserves death.

Brutus. Or let us stand to our authority,
Or let us lose it. We do here pronounce,
Upon the part o' th' people, in whose power
We were elected theirs, Marcius is worthy   210
Of present death.

Sicinius.   Therefore lay hold of him;
Bear him to th' rock Tarpeian, and from thence
Into destruction cast him.

Brutus.   Ædiles, seize him!

Citizens. Yield, Marcius, yield!

Menenius.   Hear me one word;
Beseech you, tribunes, hear me but a word.

Ædiles. Peace, peace!

Menenius. [*to Brutus*] Be that you seem, truly your
          country's friend,
And temp'rately proceed to what you would
Thus violently redress.

Brutus.   Sir, those cold ways,
That seem like prudent helps, are very poisonous   220
Where the disease is violent. Lay hands upon him,
And bear him to the rock.

Coriolanus. ['*draws his sword*']   No, I'll die here.
There's some among you have beheld me fighting:
Come, try upon yourselves what you have seen me.
  Menenius. Down with that sword! Tribunes,
       withdraw awhile.
  Brutus. Lay hands upon him.
  Menenius.   Help Marcius, help,
You that be noble; help him, young and old!
  Citizens. Down with him, down with him!

    '*In this mutiny, the Tribunes, the Ædiles, and
          the people, are beat in*'

  Menenius. Go, get you to your house; be gone, away!
All will be naught else.
  2 Senator.   Get you gone.
230 *Coriolanus*.   Stand fast;
We have as many friends as enemies.
  Menenius. Shall it be put to that?
  1 Senator.   The gods forbid!
I prithee, noble friend, home to thy house;
Leave us to cure this cause.
  Menenius.   For 'tis a sore upon us
You cannot tent yourself: be gone, beseech you.
  Cominius. Come, sir, along with us.
  Coriolanus. I would they were barbarians, as
       they are,
Though in Rome littered; not Romans, as they
       are not,
Though calved i' th' porch o' th' Capitol.
  Menenius.   Be gone.
240 Put not your worthy rage into your tongue:
One time will owe another.
  Coriolanus.   On fair ground
I could beat forty of them.

Menenius.   I could myself
Take up a brace o' th' best of them; yea, the two tribunes.
  Cominius. But now 'tis odds beyond arithmetic;
And manhood is called foolery when it stands
Against a falling fabric. Will you hence
Before the tag return? whose rage doth rend
Like interrupted waters, and o'erbear
What they are used to bear.
  Menenius.   Pray you, be gone.
I'll try whether my old wit be in request   250
With those that have but little: this must be patched
With cloth of any colour.
  Cominius. [*to Coriolanus*]   Nay, come away.
                    [*Coriolanus and Cominius depart*
 1 *Patrician.* This man has marred his fortune.
  Menenius. His nature is too noble for the world:
He would not flatter Neptune for his trident,
Or Jove for 's power to thunder. His heart's his mouth:
What his breast forges, that his tongue must vent;
And, being angry, does forget that ever
He heard the name of death.   [*noise of the people
Here's goodly work!   returning
 2 *Patrician.*   I would they were a-bed!   260
  Menenius. I would they were in Tiber! What the
          vengeance,
Could he not speak 'em fair?

'*Enter* BRUTUS *and* SICINIUS, *with the rabble again*'

  Sicinius.   Where is this viper
That would depopulate the city and
Be every man himself?
  Menenius.   You worthy tribunes—
  Sicinius. He shall be thrown down the Tarpeian rock
With rigorous hands: he hath resisted law,

And therefore law shall scorn him further trial
Than the severity of the public power,
Which he so sets at nought.

    1 Citizen.   He shall well know

270 The noble tribunes are the people's mouths,
And we their hands.

    All the citizens. He shall, sure on't.

    Menenius.   Sir, sir—

    Sicinius. Peace!

    Menenius. Do not cry havoc, where you should
        but hunt
With modest warrant.

    Sicinius.   Sir, how comes't that you
Have holp to make this rescue?

    Menenius.   Hear me speak:
As I do know the consul's worthiness,
So can I name his faults.

    Sicinius.   Consul! what consul?

    Menenius. The consul Coriolanus.

    Brutus.   He consul!

    All the citizens. No, no, no, no, no.

    Menenius. If, by the tribunes' leave, and yours,

280   good people,
I may be heard, I would crave a word or two;
The which shall turn you to no further harm
Than so much loss of time.

    Sicinius.   Speak briefly then;
For we are peremptory to dispatch
This viperous traitor: to eject him hence
Were but our danger, and to keep him here
Our certain death: therefore it is decreed
He dies to-night.

    Menenius.   Now the good gods forbid
That our renownéd Rome, whose gratitude

Towards her deservéd children is enrolled   290
In Jove's own book, like an unnatural dam
Should now eat up her own!
  Sicinius. He's a disease that must be cut away.
  Menenius. O, he's a limb that has but a disease;
Mortal, to cut it off; to cure it, easy.
What has he done to Rome that's worthy death?
Killing our enemies, the blood he hath lost—
Which I dare vouch is more than that he hath
By many an ounce—he dropped it for his country;
And what is left, to lose it by his country   300
Were to us all that do't and suffer it
A brand to th' end o' th' world.
  Sicinius.   This is clean kam.
  Brutus. Merely awry: when he did love his country,
It honoured him.
  Sicinius.   The service of the foot
Being once gangrened, is not then respected
For what before it was.
  Brutus.   We'll hear no more.
Pursue him to his house and pluck him thence,
Lest his infection, being of catching nature,
Spread further.
  Menenius.   One word more, one word!
This tiger-footed rage, when it shall find   310
The harm of unscanned swiftness, will, too late,
Tie leaden pounds to's heels. Proceed by process;
Lest parties—as he is beloved—break out,
And sack great Rome with Romans.
  Brutus.   If it were so—
  Sicinius. What do ye talk?
Have we not had a taste of his obedience?
Our ædiles smote? ourselves resisted? Come!
  Menenius. Consider this: he has been bred i' th' wars

Since a' could draw a sword, and is ill schooled
320 In bolted language; meal and bran together
He throws without distinction. Give me leave,
I'll go to him, and undertake to bring him
Where he shall answer, by a lawful form,
In peace, to his utmost peril.

  1 *Senator*.   Noble tribunes,
It is the human way: the other course
Will prove too bloody; and the end of it
Unknown to the beginning.

  Sicinius.   Noble Menenius,
Be you then as the people's officer.
Masters, lay down your weapons.

  Brutus.   Go not home.
330 *Sicinius*. Meet on the market-place. We'll attend
        you there:
Where, if you bring not Marcius, we'll proceed
In our first way.

  Menenius.   I'll bring him to you.
[*to the Senators*] Let me desire your company: he
        must come,
Or what is worst will follow.

  Senators.   Pray you, let's to him.
                                              [*they go*

[3. 2.]   *Rome. The house of Coriolanus*

        '*Enter* CORIOLANUS *with Nobles*'

Coriolanus. Let them pull all about mine ears;
        present me
Death on the wheel or at wild horses' heels;
Or pile ten hills on the Tarpeian rock,
That the precipitation might down stretch

Below the beam of sight; yet will I still
Be thus to them.
  A Noble.   You do the nobler.
  Coriolanus. I muse my mother
Does not approve me further, who was wont
To call them woollen vassals, things created
To buy and sell with groats; to show bare heads   10
In congregations, to yawn, be still and wonder,
When one but of my ordinance stood up
To speak of peace or war.

'Enter VOLUMNIA'

                 I talk of you:
Why did you wish me milder? would you have me
False to my nature? Rather say I play
The man I am.
  Volumnia.   O, sir, sir, sir,
I would have had you put your power well on,
Before you had worn it out.
  Coriolanus.   Let go.
  Volumnia. You might have been enough the man
      you are,
With striving less to be so: lesser had been   20
The thwartings of your dispositions, if
You had not showed them how ye were disposed
Ere they lacked power to cross you.
  Coriolanus.   Let them hang.
  Volumnia. Ay, and burn too.

'Enter MENENIUS with the Senators'

  Menenius. Come, come, you have been too rough,
      something too rough;
You must return and mend it.
  Senator.   There's no remedy,

Unless, by not so doing, our good city
Cleave in the midst and perish.

   Volumnia.　　　　　　　　　Pray be counselled:
I have a heart as little apt as yours,
30 But yet a brain that leads my use of anger
To better vantage.

   Menenius.　　　　　Well said, noble woman!
Before he should thus stoop to th' herd—but that
The violent fit o' th' time craves it as physic
For the whole state—I would put mine armour on,
Which I can scarcely bear.

   Coriolanus.　　　　　　　　What must I do?

   Menenius. Return to th' tribunes.

   Coriolanus.　　　　　　Well, what then? what then?

   Menenius. Repent what you have spoke.

   Coriolanus. For them! I cannot do it to the gods;
Must I then do't to them?

   Volumnia.　　　　　　　You are too absolute;
40 Though therein you can never be too noble
But when extremities speak. I have heard you say,
Honour and policy, like unsevered friends,
I' th' war do grow together: grant that, and tell me
In peace what each of them by th' other lose
That they combine not there.

   Coriolanus.　　　　　　　　Tush, tush!

   Menenius.　　　　　　　　　A good demand.

   Volumnia. If it be honour in your wars to seem
The same you are not, which for your best ends
You adopt your policy, how is it less or worse
That it shall hold companionship in peace
50 With honour as in war; since that to both
It stands in like request?

   Coriolanus.　　　　　　Why force you this?

   Volumnia. Because that now it lies you on to speak

To th' people, not by your own instruction,
Nor by th' matter which your heart prompts you,
But with such words that are but roted in
Your tongue, though but bastards and syllables
Of no allowance to your bosom's truth.
Now, this no more dishonours you at all
Than to take in a town with gentle words,
Which else would put you to your fortune and   60
The hazard of much blood.
I would dissemble with my nature, where
My fortunes and my friends at stake required
I should do so in honour. I am in this,
Your wife, your son, these senators, the nobles;
And you will rather show our general louts
How you can frown than spend a fawn upon 'em
For the inheritance of their loves and safeguard
Of what that want might ruin.
    Menenius.   Noble lady!
Come, go with us; speak fair: you may salve so,   70
Not what is dangerous present, but the loss
Of what is past.
    Volumnia.   I prithee now, my son,
Go to them with this bonnet in thy hand;
And thus far having stretched it—here be with them—
Thy knee bussing the stones: for in such business
Action is eloquence, and the eyes of th' ignorant
More learnéd than the ears—waving thy head,
Which often thus correcting thy stout heart,
Now humble as the ripest mulberry
†That will not hold the handling: or say to them,   80
Thou art their soldier, and being bred in broils
Hast not the soft way which, thou dost confess,
Were fit for thee to use, as they to claim,
In asking their good loves; but thou wilt frame

Thyself, forsooth, hereafter theirs, so far
As thou hast power and person.
Menenius.   This but done,
Even as she speaks, why, their hearts were yours;
For they have pardons, being asked, as free
As words to little purpose.
Volumnia.   Prithee now,
90 Go, and be ruled: although I know thou hadst rather
Follow thine enemy in a fiery gulf
Than flatter him in a bower.

                    '*Enter COMINIUS*'

                         Here is Cominius.
Cominius. I have been i' th' market-place; and, sir,
          'tis fit
You make strong party, or defend yourself
By calmness or by absence: all's in anger.
Menenius. Only fair speech.
Cominius.   I think 'twill serve, if he
Can thereto frame his spirit.
Volumnia.   He must, and will.
Prithee now, say you will, and go about it.
Coriolanus. Must I go show them my un-
          barbéd sconce?
100 With my base tongue give to my noble heart
A lie that it must bear? Well, I will do't:
Yet, were there but this single plot to lose,
This mould of Marcius, they to dust should grind it,
And throw't against the wind. To th' market-place!
You have put me now to such a part which never
I shall discharge to th' life.
Cominius.   Come, come, we'll prompt you.
Volumnia. I prithee now, sweet son, as thou
          hast said

My praises made thee first a soldier, so,
To have my praise for this, perform a part
Thou hast not done before.
Coriolanus.   Well, I must do't.   110
Away, my disposition, and possess me
Some harlot's spirit! My throat of war be turned,
Which choiréd with my drum, into a pipe
Small as an eunuch or the virgin voice
That babies lulls asleep! The smiles of knaves
Tent in my cheeks, and schoolboys' tears take up
The glasses of my sight! A beggar's tongue
Make motion through my lips, and my armed knees,
Who bowed but in my stirrup, bend like his
That hath received an alms! I will not do't;   120
Lest I surcease to honour mine own truth,
And by my body's action teach my mind
A most inherent baseness.
Volumnia.   At thy choice then.
To beg of thee, it is my more dishonour
Than thou of them. Come all to ruin: let
Thy mother rather feel thy pride than fear
Thy dangerous stoutness, for I mock at death
With as big heart as thou. Do as thou list.
Thy valiantness was mine, thou suck'dst it from me,
But owe thy pride thyself.
Coriolanus.   Pray, be content: 130
Mother, I am going to the market-place;
Chide me no more. I'll mountebank their loves,
Cog their hearts from them, and come home beloved
Of all the trades in Rome. Look, I am going:
Commend me to my wife. I'll return consul;
Or never trust to what my tongue can do
I' th' way of flattery further.
Volumnia.   Do your will.   [*she goes*

Cominius.　Away! the tribunes do attend you.
　　　Arm yourself
To answer mildly; for they are prepared
140　With accusations, as I hear, more strong
Than are upon you yet.
　　　Coriolanus.　The word is 'mildly.' Pray you, let us go.
Let them accuse me by invention, I
Will answer in mine honour.
　　　Menenius.　　　　　　　Ay, but mildly.
　　　Coriolanus.　Well, mildly be it then—mildly.
　　　　　　　　　　　　　　　　　　　　　　　[they go

[3. 3.]　　　　*Rome. The Forum*

'*Enter* SICINIUS *and* BRUTUS'

Brutus.　In this point charge him home, that he affects
Tyrannical power. If he evade us there,
Enforce him with his envy to the people,
And that the spoil got on the Antiates
Was ne'er distributed.

'*Enter an Ædile*'

　　　　　　　　　　　　　　What, will he come?
　　　Ædile.　He's coming.
　　　Brutus.　　　　　　　How accompanied?
　　　Ædile.　With old Menenius and those senators
That always favoured him.
　　　Sicinius.　　　　　　Have you a catalogue
Of all the voices that we have procured,
10　Set down by th' poll?
　　　Ædile.　　　　　　I have; 'tis ready.
　　　Sicinius.　Have you collected them by tribes?
　　　Ædile.　　　　　　　　　　　　I have.

Sicinius. Assemble presently the people hither:
And when they hear me say 'It shall be so
I' th' right and strength o' th' commons,' be it either
For death, for fine, or banishment, then let them,
If I say 'Fine', cry 'Fine!' if 'Death', cry 'Death!'
Insisting on the old prerogative
And power i' th' truth o' th' cause.
Ædile.   I shall inform them.
Brutus. And when such time they have begun
        to cry,
Let them not cease, but with a din confused   20
Enforce the present execution
Of what we chance to sentence.
Ædile.   Very well.
Sicinius. Make them be strong, and ready for
        this hint,
When we shall hap to give't them.
Brutus.   Go about it. [*the Ædile goes*
Put him to choler straight. He hath been used
Ever to conquer and to have his worth
Of contradiction: being once chafed, he cannot
Be reined again to temperance; then he speaks
What's in his heart; and that is there which looks
With us to break his neck.
Sicinius.   Well, here he comes.   30

'*Enter* CORIOLANUS, MENENIUS, *and* COMINIUS,
        with Senators and Patricians'

Menenius. Calmly, I do beseech you.
(*Coriolanus.* Ay, as an ostler, that for th' poorest piece
Will bear the knave by th' volume. [*aloud*] Th'
        honoured gods
Keep Rome in safety, and the chairs of justice
Supplied with worthy men! plant love among 's!

Throng our large temples with the shows of peace,
And not our streets with war!

   1 *Senator.*   Amen, amen.

   Menenius. A noble wish.

       '*Enter the Ædile, with the Plebeians*'

   Sicinius. Draw near, ye people.

40   *Ædile.* List to your tribunes. Audience! peace,
      I say!

   Coriolanus. First, hear me speak.

   Both Tribunes.   Well, say. Peace, ho!

   Coriolanus. Shall I be charged no further than
      this present?

Must all determine here?

   Sicinius.   I do demand,
If you submit you to the people's voices,
Allow their officers, and are content
To suffer lawful censure for such faults
As shall be proved upon you?

   Coriolanus.   I am content.

   Menenius. Lo, citizens, he says he is content.
The warlike service he has done, consider; think
50 Upon the the wounds his body bears, which show
Like graves i' th' holy churchyard.

   Coriolanus.   Scratches with briers,
Scars to move laughter only.

   Menenius.   Consider further,
That when he speaks not like a citizen,
You find him like a soldier: do not take
His rougher accents for malicious sounds,
But, as I say, such as become a soldier
Rather than envy you.

   Cominius.   Well, well, no more.

   Coriolanus. What is the matter

That, being passed for consul with full voice,
I am so dishonoured that the very hour   60
You take it off again?
  Sicinius.   Answer to us.
  Coriolanus. Say, then: 'tis true, I ought so.
  Sicinius. We charge you, that you have contrived
     to take
From Rome all seasoned office, and to wind
Yourself into a power tyrannical;
For which you are a traitor to the people.
  Coriolanus. How! traitor!
  Menenius.   Nay, temperately! your promise.
  Coriolanus. The fires i' th' lowest hell fold in
     the people!
Call me their traitor! Thou injurious tribune!
Within thine eyes sat twenty thousand deaths,   70
In thy hands clutched as many millions, in
Thy lying tongue both numbers, I would say
'Thou liest' unto thee with a voice as free
As I do pray the gods.
  Sicinius.   Mark you this, people?
  Citizens. To th' rock, to th' rock with him!
  Sicinius.   Peace!
We need not put new matter to his charge.
What you have seen him do and heard him speak,
Beating your officers, cursing yourselves,
Opposing laws with strokes, and here defying
Those whose great power must try him—even this,   80
So criminal and in such capital kind,
Deserves th' extremest death.
  Brutus.   But since he hath
Served well for Rome—
  Coriolanus.   What do you prate of service?
  Brutus. I talk of that that know it.

Coriolanus. You!

Menenius. Is this the promise that you made
    your mother?

Cominius. Know, I pray you—

Coriolanus.   I'll know no further.
Let them pronounce the steep Tarpeian death,
Vagabond exile, flaying, pent to linger
90 But with a grain a day, I would not buy
Their mercy at the price of one fair word,
Nor check my courage for what they can give,
To have't with saying 'Good morrow.'

Sicinius.   For that he has
(As much as in him lies) from time to time
Envied against the people, seeking means
To pluck away their power, as now at last
Given hostile strokes, and that not in the presence
Of dreaded justice, but on the ministers
That do distribute it—in the name o' th' people,
100 And in the power of us the tribunes, we,
Even from this instant, banish him our city,
In peril of precipitation
From off the rock Tarpeian, never more
To enter our Rome gates. I' th' people's name,
I say it shall be so.

Citizens. It shall be so, it shall be so! Let him away!
He's banished, and it shall be so.

Cominius. Hear me, my masters and my
    common friends—

Sicinius. He's sentenced; no more hearing.

Cominius.   Let me speak.
110 I have been consul, and can show for Rome
Her enemies' marks upon me. I do love
My country's good with a respect more tender,
More holy and profound, than mine own life,

My dear wife's estimate, her womb's increase
And treasure of my loins; then if I would
Speak that—
　　Sicinius.　We know your drift. Speak what?
　　Brutus.　There's no more to be said, but he
　　　is banished
As enemy to the people and his country.
It shall be so.
　　Citizens.　It shall be so, it shall be so.
　　Coriolanus.　You common cry of curs! whose
　　　breath I hate　　　　　　　　　　　　　　120
As reek o' th' rotten fens, whose loves I prize
As the dead carcasses of unburied men
That do corrupt my air—I banish you.
And here remain with your uncertainty!
Let every feeble rumour shake your hearts!
Your enemies, with nodding of their plumes,
Fan you into despair! Have the power still
To banish your defenders, till at length
Your ignorance—which finds not till it feels,
Making but reservation of yourselves,　　　　130
Still your own foes—deliver you as most
Abated captives to some nation
That won you without blows! Despising
For you the city, thus I turn my back:
There is a world elsewhere.
　　　　　　　[*he goes, followed by Cominius, Menenius,*
　　　　　　　　　　　　　Senators and Patricians

　　Ædile.　The people's enemy is gone, is gone!
　　Citizens.　Our enemy is banished! he is gone!
　　　Hoo—oo! [*'they all shout, and throw up their*
　　　　　　　　　　　　　　　　　　　　　　　caps'
　　Sicinius.　Go see him out at gates, and follow him,
As he hath followed you, with all despite;

140 Give him deserved vexation. Let a guard
    Attend us through the city.
        Citizens. Come, come, let's see him out at
            gates; come!
    The gods preserve our noble tribunes! Come.   [*they go*

[4. 1.]   *Rome. Before a gate of the city*

'*Enter* CORIOLANUS, VOLUMNIA, VIRGILIA, MENENIUS,
    COMINIUS, *with the young Nobility of Rome*'

    Coriolanus. Come, leave your tears; a brief farewell!
            The beast
    With many heads butts me away. Nay, mother,
    Where is your ancient courage? you were used
    To say extremity was the trier of spirits;
    That common chances common men could bear;
    That when the sea was calm all boats alike
    Showed mastership in floating; fortune's blows,
    When most struck home, being gentle wounded, craves
    A noble cunning. You were used to load me
  10 With precepts that would make invincible
    The heart that conned them.
        Virgilia. O heavens! O heavens!
        Coriolanus.   Nay, I prithee, woman—
        Volumnia. Now the red pestilence strike all trades
            in Rome,
    And occupations perish!
        Coriolanus.   What, what, what!
    I shall be loved when I am lacked. Nay, mother,
    Resume that spirit when you were wont to say,
    If you had been the wife of Hercules,
    Six of his labours you'ld have done, and saved

Your husband so much sweat. Cominius,
Droop not; adieu. Farewell, my wife, my mother: 20
I'll do well yet. Thou old and true Menenius,
Thy tears are salter than a younger man's,
And venomous to thine eyes. My sometime general,
I have seen thee stern, and thou hast oft beheld
Heart-hard'ning spectacles; tell these sad women
'Tis fond to wail inevitable strokes,
As 'tis to laugh at 'em. Mother, you wot well
My hazards still have been your solace: and
Believe't not lightly—though I go alone,
Like to a lonely dragon, that his fen   30
Makes feared and talked of more than seen—your son
Will or exceed the common or be caught
With cautelous baits and practice.
　Volumnia.　　　　　　　My first son,
Whither wilt thou go? Take good Cominius
With thee awhile: determine on some course
More than a wild exposure to each chance
That starts i' th' way before thee.
　Virgilia　　　　　　　O the gods!
　Cominius. I'll follow thee a month, devise with thee
Where thou shalt rest, that thou mayst hear of us
And we of thee: so, if the time thrust forth   40
A cause for thy repeal, we shall not send
O'er the vast world to seek a single man,
And lose advantage, which doth ever cool
I' th' absence of the needer.
　Coriolanus.　　　　　　Fare ye well:
Thou hast years upon thee; and thou art too full
Of the wars' surfeits to go rove with one
That's yet unbruised: bring me but out at gate.
Come, my sweet wife, my dearest mother, and
My friends of noble touch; when I am forth,

50 Bid me farewell, and smile. I pray you, come.
While I remain above the ground you shall
Hear from me still, and never of me aught
But what is like me formerly.

Menenius.   That's worthily
As any ear can hear. Come, let's not weep.
If I could shake off but one seven years
From these old arms and legs, by the good gods,
I'ld with thee every foot.

Coriolanus.   Give me thy hand.
Come.   *[they go*

[4. 2.]   *Rome. A street near the gate*

'*Enter the two Tribunes,* SICINIUS *and* BRUTUS,
with the Ædile'

Sicinius Bid them all home; he's gone, and we'll
    no further.
The nobility are vexed, whom we see have sided
In his behalf.

Brutus.   Now we have shown our power,
Let us seem humbler after it is done
Than when it was a-doing.

Sicinius.   Bid them home:
Say their great enemy is gone, and they
Stand in their ancient strength.

Brutus.   Dismiss them home. *[the Ædile goes*
Here comes his mother.

'*Enter* VOLUMNIA, VIRGILIA, *and* MENENIUS'

Sicinius.   Let's not meet her.
Brutus.   Why?

Sicinius. They say she's mad.

Brutus. They have ta'en note of us: keep on
    your way.   10

Volumnia. O, you're well met: th' hoarded plague
    o' th' gods
Requite your love!

Menenius.   Peace, peace, be not so loud.

Volumnia. If that I could for weeping, you
    should hear—
Nay, and you shall hear some. [*to Brutus*] Will you
    be gone?

Virgilia. [*to Sicinius*] You shall stay too. I would
    I had the power
To say so to my husband.

Sicinius.   Are you mankind?

Volumnia. Ay, fool; is that a shame? Note but
    this, fool.
Was not a man my father? Hadst thou foxship
To banish him that struck more blows for Rome
Than thou hast spoken words?

Sicinius.   O blessed heavens!   20

Volumnia. Moe noble blows than ever thou
    wise words;
And for Rome's good. I'll tell thee what—yet go!
Nay, but thou shalt stay too. I would my son
Were in Arabia, and thy tribe before him,
His good sword in his hand.

Sicinius.   What then?

Virgilia.   What then!
He'ld make an end of thy posterity.

Volumnia. Bastards and all.
Good man, the wounds that he does bear for Rome!

Menenius. Come, come, peace.

Sicinius. I would he had continued to his country   30

As he began, and not unknit himself
The noble knot he made.
   Brutus.   I would he had.
   Volumnia. 'I would he had!' 'Twas you incensed
      the rabble;
Cats, that can judge as fitly of his worth
As I can of those mysteries which heaven
Will not have earth to know.
   Brutus.   Pray, let's go.
   Volumnia. Now, pray, sir, get you gone;
You have done a brave deed. Ere you go, hear this:
As far as doth the Capitol exceed
40 The meanest house in Rome, so far my son—
This lady's husband here, this, do you see?
Whom you have banished—does exceed you all.
   Brutus. Well, well, we'll leave you.
   Sicinius.   Why stay we to be baited
With one that wants her wits?
   Volumnia.   Take my prayers with you.
                                  [Tribunes go
I would the gods had nothing else to do
But to confirm my curses! Could I meet 'em
But once a day, it would unclog my heart
Of what lies heavy to't.
   Menenius.   You have told them home,
And by my troth you have cause. You'll sup with me?
50   *Volumnia.* Anger's my meat; I sup upon myself,
And so shall starve with feeding. Come, let's go:
Leave this faint puling, and lament as I do,
In anger, Juno-like. Come, come, come.
                      [Vol. and Vir. depart
   Menenius. Fie, fie, fie!   *[he follows*

[4. 3.]   *A highway between Rome and Antium*

'Enter a Roman and a Volsce', meeting

Roman. I know you well, sir, and you know me: your name, I think, is Adrian.

Volsce. It is so, sir: truly, I have forgot you.

Roman. I am a Roman; and my services are, as you are, against 'em. Know you me yet?

Volsce. Nicanor? no.

Roman. The same, sir.

Volsce. You had more beard when I last saw you; but your favour is well approved by your tongue. What's the news in Rome? I have a note from the Volscian 10 state to find you out there: you have well saved me a day's journey.

Roman. There hath been in Rome strange insurrections; the people against the senators, patricians, and nobles.

Volsce. Hath been! is it ended then? Our state thinks not so: they are in a most warlike preparation, and hope to come upon them in the heat of their division.

Roman. The main blaze of it is past, but a small thing 20 would make it flame again; for the nobles receive so to heart the banishment of that worthy Coriolanus, that they are in a ripe aptness to take all power from the people and to pluck from them their tribunes for ever. This lies glowing, I can tell you, and is almost mature for the violent breaking out.

Volsce. Coriolanus banished!

Roman. Banished, sir.

Volsce. You will be welcome with this intelligence, Nicanor.   30

Roman. The day serves well for them now. I have heard it said the fittest time to corrupt a man's wife is when she's fall'n out with her husband. Your noble Tullus Aufidius will appear well in these wars, his great opposer, Coriolanus, being now in no request of his country.

Volsce. He cannot choose. I am most fortunate thus accidentally to encounter you: you have ended my business, and I will merrily accompany you home.

40 *Roman.* I shall, between this and supper, tell you most strange things from Rome; all tending to the good of their adversaries. Have you an army ready, say you?

Volsce. A most royal one; the centurions and their charges, distinctly billeted, already in th' entertainment, and to be on foot at an hour's warning.

Roman. I am joyful to hear of their readiness, and am the man, I think, that shall set them in present action. So, sir, heartily well met, and most glad of your 50 company.

Volsce. You take my part from me, sir; I have the most cause to be glad of yours.

Roman. Well, let us go together.　　　　[*they go*

[4. 4.]　　　*Antium. Before Aufidius's house*

'*Enter* CORIOLANUS *in mean apparel, disguised and muffled*'

Coriolanus. A goodly city is this Antium. City,
'Tis I that made thy widows: many an heir
Of these fair edifices 'fore my wars
Have I heard groan and drop. Then know me not,

Lest that thy wives with spits and boys with stones
In puny battle slay me.

'*Enter a Citizen*'

Save you, sir.

Citizen. And you.

Coriolanus.   Direct me, if it be your will,
Where great Aufidius lies. Is he in Antium?

Citizen. He is, and feasts the nobles of the state
At his house this night.

Coriolanus.   Which is his house, beseech you? 10

Citizen. This here before you.

Coriolanus.   Thank you, sir: farewell.

[*Citizen goes*

O world, thy slippery turns! Friends now fast sworn,
Whose double bosoms seem to wear one heart,
Whose hours, whose bed, whose meal and exercise
Are still together, who twin, as 'twere, in love
Unseparable, shall within this hour,
On a dissension of a doit, break out
To bitterest enmity: so fellest foes,
Whose passions and whose plots have broke their sleep
To take the one the other, by some chance,   20
Some trick not worth an egg, shall grow dear friends
And interjoin their issues. So with me:
My birth-place hate I, and my love's upon
This enemy town. I'll enter: if he slay me,
He does fair justice; if he give me way,
I'll do his country service.   [*he enters the house*

[4. 5.] *Antium. A hall in Aufidius's house, with three doors, one right leading to the outer gate, one left leading to the buttery, etc; the third centre opening into the great chamber*

'*Music plays. Enter a Servingman*' *from the chamber*

1 *Servingman.* Wine, wine, wine! What service is there!
I think our fellows are asleep.   [*goes out left*

'*Enter another Servingman*' *from the chamber*

2 *Servingman.* Where's Cotus? my master calls for him. Cotus!   [*returns*

'*Enter* CORIOLANUS' *from without*

Coriolanus. A goodly house. The feast smells well, but I
Appear not like a guest.

Re-enter 1 *Servingman with wine*

1 *Servingman.* What would you have, friend? whence are you? Here's no place for you: pray go to the door!
                                            [*returns to the chamber*
Coriolanus. I have deserved no better entertainment,
10 In being Coriolanus.

Re-enter 2 *Servingman*

2 *Servingman.* Whence are you, sir? Has the porter his eyes in his head that he gives entrance to such companions? Pray get you out.
Coriolanus. Away!
2 *Servingman.* 'Away!' Get you away.
Coriolanus. Now thou'rt troublesome.
2 *Servingman.* Are you so brave? I'll have you talked with anon.

Enter from the chamber 3 *Servingman with* 1 *Servingman*

3 *Servingman.* What fellow's this?

1 *Servingman.* A strange one as ever I looked on! 20
I cannot get him out o' th' house. Prithee call my
master to him.

3 *Servingman.* What have you to do here, fellow?
Pray you avoid the house.

Coriolanus. Let me but stand; I will not hurt your
hearth.

3 *Servingman.* What are you?

Coriolanus. A gentleman.

3 *Servingman.* A marvllous poor one.

Coriolanus. True, so I am.   30

3 *Servingman.* Pray you, poor gentleman, take up
some other station; here's no place for you. Pray you
avoid. Come.

Coriolanus. Follow your function, go and batten on
cold bits.   ['*pushes him away from him*'

3 *Servingman.* What, you will not? Prithee, tell my
master what a strange guest he has here.

2 *Servingman.* And I shall. [*returns to the chamber*

3 *Servingman.* Where dwell'st thou?

Coriolanus. Under the canopy.   40

3 *Servingman.* Under the canopy!

Coriolanus. Ay.

3 *Servingman.* Where's that?

Coriolanus. I' th' city of kites and crows.

3 *Servingman.* I' th' city of kites and crows! What
an ass it is! then thou dwell'st with daws too?

Coriolanus. No, I serve not thy master.

3 *Servingman.* How, sir! do you meddle with my
master?

Coriolanus. Ay; 'tis an honester service than to meddle 50

with thy mistress. Thou prat'st, and prat'st; serve
with thy trencher. Hence! ['*beats him*' *from the room*

Enter AUFIDIUS *with* 2 *Servingman*

Aufidius. Where is this fellow?

2 *Servingman.* Here, sir. I'ld have beaten him like
a dog, but for disturbing the lords within. [*returns*

Aufidius. Whence com'st thou? What wouldst thou?
    Thy name?
Why speak'st not? Speak, man. What's thy name?

Coriolanus. [*unmuffling*]   If, Tullus,
Not yet thou know'st me, and, seeing me, dost not
Think me for the man I am, necessity
60 Commands me name myself.

Aufidius.   What is thy name?

Coriolanus. A name unmusical to the Volscians' ears,
And harsh in sound to thine.

Aufidius.   Say, what's thy name?
Thou hast a grim appearance, and thy face
Bears a command in't; though thy tackle's torn,
Thou show'st a noble vessel. What's thy name?

Coriolanus. Prepare thy brow to frown—know'st thou
    me yet?

Aufidius. I know thee not. Thy name!

Coriolanus. My name is Caius Marcius, who
    hath done
To thee particularly, and to all the Volsces,
70 Great hurt and mischief; thereto witness may
My surname, Coriolanus. The painful service,
The extreme dangers, and the drops of blood
Shed for my thankless country, are requited
But with that surname—a good memory
And witness of the malice and displeasure
Which thou shouldst bear me. Only that name remains:

The cruelty and envy of the people,
Permitted by our dastard nobles, who
Have all forsook me, hath devoured the rest;
And suffered me by th' voice of slaves to be   80
Whooped out of Rome. Now, this extremity
Hath brought me to thy hearth: not out of hope—
Mistake me not—to save my life; for if
I had feared death, of all the men i' th' world
I would have 'voided thee; but in mere spite,
To be full quit of those my banishers,
Stand I before thee here. Then if thou hast
A heart of wreak in thee, that wilt revenge
Thine own particular wrongs and stop those maims
Of shame seen through thy country, speed thee straight 90
And make my misery serve thy turn. So use it
That my revengeful services may prove
As benefits to thee; for I will fight
Against my cank'red country with the spleen
Of all the under fiends. But if so be
Thou dar'st not this and that to prove more fortunes
Thou'rt tired, then, in a word, I also am
Longer to live most weary, and present
My throat to thee and to thy ancient malice;
Which not to cut would show thee but a fool,   100
Since I have ever followed thee with hate,
Drawn tuns of blood out of thy country's breast,
And cannot live but to thy shame, unless
It be to do thee service.
Aufidius.   O Marcius, Marcius!
Each word thou hast spoke hath weeded from my heart
A root of ancient envy. If Jupiter
Should from yond cloud speak divine things,
And say 'Tis true', I'ld not believe them more
Than thee, all noble Marcius. Let me twine

110 Mine arms about that body, where against
My grainéd ash an hundred times hath broke
And scarred the moon with splinters: here I clip
The anvil of my sword, and do contest
As hotly and as nobly with thy love
As ever in ambitious strength I did
Contend against thy valour. Know thou first,
I loved the maid I married; never man
Sighed truer breath; but that I see thee here,
Thou noble thing, more dances my rapt heart
120 Than when I first my wedded mistress saw
Bestride my threshold. Why, thou Mars, I tell thee,
We have a power on foot, and I had purpose
Once more to hew thy target from thy brawn,
Or lose mine arm for't. Thou hast beat me out
Twelve several times, and I have nightly since
Dreamt of encounters 'twixt thyself and me;
We have been down together in my sleep,
Unbuckling helms, fisting each other's throat;
And waked half dead with nothing. Worthy Marcius,
130 Had we no quarrel else to Rome but that
Thou art thence banished, we would muster all
From twelve to seventy, and pouring war
Into the bowels of ungrateful Rome,
Like a bold flood o'erbear't. O, come, go in,
And take our friendly senators by th' hands,
Who now are here, taking their leaves of me
Who am prepared against your territories,
Though not for Rome itself.
  Coriolanus.   You bless me, gods!
  Aufidius. Therefore, most absolute sir, if thou wilt have
140 The leading of thine own revenges, take
Th' one half of my commission, and set down—
As best thou art experienced, since thou know'st

Thy country's strength and weakness—thine own ways,
Whether to knock against the gates of Rome,
Or rudely visit them in parts remote
To fright them ere destroy. But come in:
Let me commend thee first to those that shall
Say yea to thy desires. A thousand welcomes!
And more a friend than e'er an enemy;
Yet, Marcius, that was much. Your hand:
    most welcome!   150
       [*leads him in. 'Enter two of the Servingmen'*

1 *Servingman*. Here's a strange alteration!

2 *Servingman*. By my hand, I had thought to have strucken him with a cudgel; and yet my mind gave me his clothes made a false report of him.

1 *Servingman*. What an arm he has! he turned me about with his finger and his thumb, as one would set up a top.

2 *Servingman*. Nay, I knew by his face that there was something in him; he had, sir, a kind of face, methought—I cannot tell how to term it.   160

1 *Servingman*. He had so, looking as it were—Would I were hanged, but I thought there was more in him than I could think.

2 *Servingman*. So did I, I'll be sworn: he is simply the rarest man i' th' world.

1 *Servingman*. I think he is; but a greater soldier than he, you wot one.

2 *Servingman*. Who, my master?

1 *Servingman*. Nay, it's no matter for that.

2 *Servingman*. Worth six on him.   170

1 *Servingman*. Nay, not so neither: but I take him to be the greater soldier.

2 *Servingman*. Faith, look you, one cannot tell how to say that: for the defence of a town our general is excellent.

1 *Servingman.* Ay, and for an assault too.

'*Enter the third Servingman*'

3 *Servingman.* O slaves, I can tell you news—news, you rascals!

1, 2 *Servingmen.* What, what, what? Let's partake.

3 *Servingman.* I would not be a Roman, of all nations; 180 I had as lief be a condemned man.

1, 2 *Servingmen.* Wherefore? wherefore?

3 *Servingman.* Why, here's he that was wont to thwack our general—Caius Marcius.

1 *Servingman.* Why do you say 'thwack our general'?

3 *Servingman.* I do not say 'thwack our general', but he was always good enough for him.

2 *Servingman.* Come, we are fellows and friends. He was ever too hard for him; I have heard him say 190 so himself.

1 *Servingman.* He was too hard for him directly. To say the troth on't, before Corioli he scotched him and notched him like a carbonado.

2 *Servingman.* An he had been cannibally given, he might have broiled and eaten him too.

1 *Servingman.* But more of thy news?

3 *Servingman.* Why, he is so made on here within as if he were son and heir to Mars; set at upper end o' th' table; no question asked him by any of the senators but 200 they stand bald before him. Our general himself makes a mistress of him; sanctifies himself with's hand, and turns up the white o' th' eye to his discourse. But the bottom of the news is, our general is cut i' th' middle and but one half of what he was yesterday, for the other has half by the entreaty and grant of the whole table. He'll go, he says, and sowl the porter of Rome gates by

th' ears; he will mow all down before him, and leave
his passage polled.

2 *Servingman.* And he's as like to do't as any man I can
imagine.   210

3 *Servingman.* Do't! he will do't; for look you, sir, he
has as many friends as enemies; which friends, sir, as it
were, durst not—look you, sir—show themselves, as we
term it, his friends whilst he's in dejectitude.

1 *Servingman.* Dejectitude! what's that?

3 *Servingman.* But when they shall see, sir, his crest
up again and the man in blood, they will out of their
burrows, like conies after rain, and revel all with him.

1 *Servingman.* But when goes this forward?

3 *Servingman.* To-morrow, to-day, presently. You 220
shall have the drum struck up this afternoon; 'tis as it
were a parcel of their feast, and to be executed ere they
wipe their lips.

2 *Servingman.* Why, then we shall have a stirring
world again. This peace is nothing but to rust iron,
increase tailors, and breed ballad-makers.

1 *Servingman.* Let me have war, say I; it exceeds
peace as far as day does night; it's sprightly, waking,
audible, and full of vent. Peace is a very apoplexy,
lethargy; mulled, deaf, sleepy, insensible; a getter of 230
more bastard children than war's a destroyer of men.

2 *Servingman.* 'Tis so: and as war in some sort may be
said to be a ravisher, so it cannot be denied but peace is
a great maker of cuckolds.

1 *Servingman.* Ay, and it makes men hate one another.

3 *Servingman.* Reason: because they then less need
one another. The wars for my money. I hope to see
Romans as cheap as Volscians. They are rising, they are
rising.

1, 2 *Servingmen.* In, in, in, in!   [*they hasten in* 240

[4. 6.]   *Rome.   A public place*

'*Enter the two Tribunes,* SICINIUS *and* BRUTUS'

Sicinius. We hear not of him, neither need we
        fear him.
His remedies are tame. The present peace
And quietness of the people, which before
Were in wild hurry, here do make his friends
Blush that the world goes well; who rather had,
Though they themselves did suffer by't, behold
Dissentious numbers pest'ring streets than see
Our tradesmen singing in their shops, and going
About their functions friendly.
10   *Brutus.* We stood to't in good time.

'*Enter* MENENIUS'

                              Is this Menenius?
Sicinius. 'Tis he, 'tis he. O, he is grown most kind
Of late. Hail, sir!
Menenius.   Hail to you both!
Sicinius. Your Coriolanus is not much missed
But with his friends. The commonwealth doth stand,
And so would do, were he more angry at it.
Menenius. All's well; and might have been much
        better, if
He could have temporized.
Sicinius.   Where is he, hear you?
Menenius. Nay, I hear nothing: his mother and
        his wife
Hear nothing from him.

'*Enter three or four Citizens*'

Citizens. The gods preserve you both!

Sicinius.   God-den, our neighbours. 20
Brutus. God-den to you all, god-den to you all.
1 *Citizen.* Ourselves, our wives, and children, on
    our knees,
Are bound to pray for you both.
Sicinius.   Live, and thrive!
Brutus. Farewell, kind neighbours: we
    wished Coriolanus
Had loved you as we did.
Citizens.   Now the gods keep you!
Both Tribunes. Farewell, farewell. [*Citizens pass on*
Sicinius. This is a happier and more comely time
Than when these fellows ran about the streets
Crying confusion.
Brutus.   Caius Marcius was
A worthy officer i' th' war, but insolent,   30
O'ercome with pride, ambitious past all thinking,
Self-loving—
Sicinius. And affecting one sole throne,
Without assistance.
Menenius.   I think not so.
Sicinius. We should by this, to all our lamentation,
If he had gone forth consul, found it so.
Brutus. The gods have well prevented it, and Rome
Sits safe and still without him.

'*Enter an Ædile*'

Ædile.   Worthy tribunes,
There is a slave, whom we have put in prison,
Reports the Volsces with two several powers
Are ent'red in the Roman territories,   40
And with the deepest malice of the war
Destroy what lies before 'em.
Menenius.   'Tis Aufidius,

Who, hearing of our Marcius' banishment,
Thrusts forth his horns again into the world,
Which were inshelled when Marcius stood for Rome,
And durst not once peep out.
    Sicinius.   Come, what talk you
Of Marcius?
    Brutus. Go see this rumourer whipped. It cannot be
The Volsces dare break with us.
    Menenius.   Cannot be!
50 We have record that very well it can;
And three examples of the like hath been
Within my age. But reason with the fellow,
Before you punish him, where he heard this,
Lest you shall chance to whip your information
And beat the messenger who bids beware
Of what is to be dreaded.
    Sicinius.   Tell not me:
I know this cannot be.
    Brutus.   Not possible.

            'Enter a Messenger'

    Messenger. The nobles in great earnestness
              are going
All to the Senate House: some news is come
60 That turns their countenances.
    Sicinius.   'Tis this slave—
Go whip him 'fore the people's eyes—his raising,
Nothing but his report.
    Messenger.   Yes, worthy sir,
The slave's report is seconded; and more,
More fearful, is delivered.
    Sicinius.   What more fearful?
    Messenger. It is spoke freely out of many mouths—
How probable I do not know—that Marcius,

Joined with Aufidius, leads a power 'gainst Rome,
And vows revenge as spacious as between
The young'st and oldest thing.
　　Sicinius　　　　　　　This is most likely!
　　Brutus. Raised only that the weaker sort may wish　70
Good Marcius home again.
　　Sicinius.　　　　　　　The very trick on't.
　　Menenius. This is unlikely:
He and Aufidius can no more atone
Than violent'st contrarieties.

Enter a second Messenger

　　2 Messenger. You are sent for to the Senate.
A fearful army, led by Caius Marcius
Associated with Aufidius, rages
Upon our territories, and have already
O'erborne their way, consumed with fire, and took
What lay before them.　　　　　　　　80

'*Enter* COMINIUS'

　　Cominius. O, you have made good work!
　　Menenius.　　　　　　　What news? what news?
　　Cominius. You have holp to ravish your own
　　　daughters and
To melt the city leads upon your pates,
To see your wives dishonoured to your noses—
　　Menenius. What's the news? what's the news?
　　Cominius. Your temples burnéd in their cement, and
Your franchises, whereon you stood, confined
Into an auger's bore.
　　Menenius.　　　　Pray now, your news?—
You have made fair work, I fear me.—Pray, your news?—　90
If Marcius should be joined wi'th' Volscians—
　　Cominius.　　　　　　　　　　If!

He is their god; he leads them like a thing
Made by some other deity than Nature,
That shapes man better; and they follow him
Against us brats with no less confidence
Than boys pursuing summer butterflies,
Or butchers killing flies.

  Menenius.   You have made good work,
You and your apron-men; you that stood so much
Upon the voice of occupation and
The breath of garlic-eaters!

  Cominius.   He will shake
100 Your Rome about your ears.

  Menenius.   As Hercules
Did shake down mellow fruit. You have made
     fair work!

  Brutus. But is this true, sir?

  Cominius.   Ay; and you'll look pale
Before you find it other. All the regions
Do smilingly revolt, and who resist
Are mocked for valiant ignorance,
And perish constant fools. Who is't can blame him?
Your enemies and his find something in him.

  Menenius. We are all undone, unless
The noble man have mercy.

  Cominius.   Who shall ask it?
110 The tribunes cannot do't for shame; the people
Deserve such pity of him as the wolf
Does of the shepherds; for his best friends, if they
Should say 'Be good to Rome,' they charged
     him even
As those should do that had deserved his hate,
And therein showed like enemies.

  Menenius.   'Tis true:
If he were putting to my house the brand

That should consume it, I have not the face
To say 'Beseech you, cease.' You have made
  fair hands,
You and your crafts! you have crafted fair!
 Cominius.   You have brought
A trembling upon Rome, such as was never   120
S' incapable of help.
 Both Tribunes. Say not we brought it.
 Menenius. How! Was't we? We loved him, but,
  like beasts
And cowardly nobles, gave way unto your clusters,
Who did hoot him out o' th' city.
 Cominius.   But I fear
They'll roar him in again. Tullus Aufidius,
The second name of men, obeys his points
As if he were his officer. Desperation
Is all the policy, strength, and defence,
That Rome can make against them.

   'Enter a troop of Citizens'

 Menenius.   Here come the clusters.
And is Aufidius with him? You are they   130
That made the air unwholesome when you cast
Your stinking greasy caps in hooting at
Coriolanus' exile. Now he's coming,
And not a hair upon a soldier's head
Which will not prove a whip; as many coxcombs
As you threw caps up will he tumble down,
And pay you for your voices. 'Tis no matter;
If he could burn us all into one coal,
We have deserved it.
 Citizens. Faith, we hear fearful news.
 1 Citizen.   For mine own part, 140
When I said banish him, I said 'twas pity.

2 *Citizen.* And so did I.

3 *Citizen.* And so did I; and, to say the truth, so did
very many of us. That we did, we did for the best; and
though we willingly consented to his banishment, yet
it was against our will.

Cominius. You're goodly things, you voices!

Menenius.   You have made
Good work, you and your cry! Shall's to the Capitol?

Cominius. O, ay, what else?

                              [*Cominius and Menenius go*

150   *Sicinius.* Go masters, get you home; be not dismayed;
These are a side that would be glad to have
This true which they so seem to fear. Go home,
And show no sign of fear.

1 *Citizen.* The gods be good to us! Come, masters,
let's home. I ever said we were i'th' wrong when we
banished him.

2 *Citizen.* So did we all. But come, let's home.

                              [*Citizens disperse*

Brutus. I do not like this news.

Sicinius. Nor I.

160   *Brutus.* Let's to the Capitol. Would half my wealth
Would buy this for a lie!

Sicinius.   Pray, let us go.   [*they go*

[4.7.]   *A camp at a small distance from Rome*

        '*Enter* AUFIDIUS *with his Lieutenant*'

Aufidius. Do they still fly to th' Roman?

Lieutenant. I do not know what witchcraft's in
        him, but
Your soldiers use him as the grace 'fore meat,
Their talk at table and their thanks at end;

And you are dark'ned in this action sir,
Even by your own.
  Aufidius.   I cannot help it now,
Unless by using means I lame the foot
Of our design. He bears himself more proudlier,
Even to my person, than I thought he would
When first I did embrace him; yet his nature   10
In that's no changeling, and I must excuse
What cannot be amended.
  Lieutenant.   Yet I wish, sir—
I mean for your particular—you had not
Joined in commission with him, but either
Had borne the action of yourself, or else
To him had left it solely.
  Aufidius. I understand thee well; and be thou sure,
When he shall come to his account, he knows not
What I can urge against him. Although it seems,
And so he thinks, and is no less apparent   20
To th' vulgar eye, that he bears all things fairly
And shows good husbandry for the Volscian state,
Fights dragon-like, and does achieve as soon
As draw his sword; yet he hath left undone
That which shall break his neck or hazard mine,
Whene'er we come to our account.
  Lieutenant. Sir, I beseech you, think you he'll
     carry Rome?
  Aufidius. All places yield to him ere he sits down,
And the nobility of Rome are his;
The senators and patricians love him too.   30
The tribunes are no soldiers, and their people
Will be as rash in the repeal, as hasty
To expel him thence. I think he'll be to Rome
As is the osprey to the fish, who takes it
By sovereignty of nature. First he was

A noble servant to them, but he could not
Carry his honours even. Whether 'twas pride,
Which out of daily fortune ever taints
The happy man; whether defect of judgement,
40 To fail in the disposing of those chances
Which he was lord of; or whether nature,
Not to be other than one thing, not moving
From th' casque to th' cushion, but commanding peace
Even with the same austerity and garb
As he controlled the war; but one of these—
As he hath spices of them all—not all,
For I dare so far free him—made him feared,
So hated, and so banished: but he has a merit
To choke it in the utt'rance. So our virtues
50 Lie in th' interpretation of the time;
And power, unto itself most commendable,
Hath not a tomb so evident as a chair
T' extol what it hath done.
One fire drives out one fire; one nail, one nail;
Rights by rights fouler, strengths by strengths do fail.
Come, let's away. When, Caius, Rome is thine,
Thou art poor'st of all; then shortly art thou mine.

                                                [they go

[5. 1.]   Rome. A public place

'Enter MENENIUS, COMINIUS, SICINIUS, BRUTUS,
        the two Tribunes, with others'

Menenius. No, I'll not go: you hear what he
            hath said
Which was sometime his general, who loved him
In a most dear particular. He called me father;
But what o' that? Go you that banished him,

A mile before his tent fall down, and knee
The way into his mercy. Nay, if he coyed
To hear Cominius speak, I'll keep at home.
  Cominius. He would not seem to know me.
  Menenius.   Do you hear?
  Cominius. Yet one time he did call me by my name.
I urged our old acquaintance, and the drops   10
That we have bled together. 'Coriolanus'
He would not answer to; forbad all names;
He was a kind of nothing, titleless,
Till he had forged himself a name i' th' fire
Of burning Rome.
  Menenius.   Why, so! You have made good work!
A pair of tribunes that have wrecked fair Rome
To make coals cheap—a noble memory!
  Cominius. I minded him how royal 'twas to pardon
When it was less expected; he replied,
It was a bare petition of a state   20
To one whom they had punished.
  Menenius.   Very well.
Could he say less?
  Cominius. I offered to awaken his regard
For 's private friends: his answer to me was,
He could not stay to pick them in a pile
Of noisome musty chaff. He said 'twas folly,
For one poor grain or two, to leave unburnt
And still to nose th' offence.
  Menenius.   For one poor grain or two!
I am one of those; his mother, wife, his child,
And this brave fellow too, we are the grains: 30
You are the musty chaff, and you are smelt
Above the moon. We must be burnt for you.
  Sicinius. Nay, pray, be patient: if you refuse your aid
In this so never-needed help, yet do not

Upbraid's with our distress. But, sure, if you
Would be your country's pleader, your good tongue,
More than the instant army we can make,
Might stop our countryman.

    Menenius.   No, I'll not meddle.

    Sicinius. Pray you, go to him.

    Menenius.   What should I do?

40 *Brutus.* Only make trial what your love can do
For Rome, towards Marcius.

    Menenius.   Well, and say that Marcius
Return me, as Cominius is returned,
Unheard—what then?
But as a discontented friend, grief-shot
With his unkindness? Say 't be so?

    Sicinius.   Yet your good will
Must have that thanks from Rome after the measure
As you intended well.

    Menenius.   I'll undertake 't:
I think he'll hear me. Yet to bite his lip
And hum at good Cominius much unhearts me.

50 He was not taken well; he had not dined:
The veins unfilled, our blood is cold, and then
We pout upon the morning, are unapt
To give or to forgive; but when we have stuffed
These pipes and these conveyances of our blood
With wine and feeding, we have suppler souls
Than in our priest-like fasts: therefore I'll watch him
Till he be dieted to my request,
And then I'll set upon him.

    Brutus. You know the very road into his kindness,

60 And cannot lose your way.

    Menenius.   Good faith, I'll prove him,
Speed how it will. I shall ere long have knowledge
Of my success.   *[goes*

Cominius.   He'll never hear him.

Sicinius.   Not?

Cominius. I tell you he does sit in gold, his eye
Red as 'twould burn Rome, and his injury
The gaoler to his pity. I kneeled before him;
'Twas very faintly he said 'Rise;' dismissed me
Thus with his speechless hand. What he would do
†He sent in writing after me; what he would not,
†Bound with an oath to yield to his conditions:
So that all hope is vain,   70
Unless his noble mother, and his wife—
Who, as I hear, mean to solicit him
For mercy to his country. Therefore, let's hence,
And with our fair entreaties haste them on.

                                                        [*they go*

[5. 2.]   *Entrance of the Volscian camp before Rome*

        '*Enter* MENENIUS *to the Watch on Guard*'

  1 *Watch.* Stay. Whence are you?

  2 *Watch.*   Stand, and go back.

Menenius. You guard like men, 'tis well; but, by
        your leave,
I am an officer of state, and come
To speak with Coriolanus.

  1 *Watch.*   From whence?

Menenius.   From Rome.

  1 *Watch.* You may not pass, you must return:
        our general
Will no more hear from thence.

  2 *Watch.* You'll see your Rome embraced with
        fire, before
You'll speak with Coriolanus.

Menenius. Good my friends,
If you have heard your general talk of Rome
10 And of his friends there, it is lots to blanks
My name hath touched your ears: it is Menenius.

1 *Watch.* Be it so; go back. The virtue of
    your name
Is not here passable.

Menenius. I tell thee, fellow,
Thy general is my lover. I have been
The book of his good acts whence men have read
His fame unparalleled—haply amplified;
For I have ever varnishéd my friends
(Of whom he's chief) with all the size that verity
Would without lapsing suffer: nay, sometimes,
20 Like to a bowl upon a subtle ground,
I have tumbled past the throw, and in his praise
Have almost stamped the leasing: therefore, fellow,
I must have leave to pass.

1 *Watch.* Faith, sir, if you had told as many lies in his
behalf as you have uttered words in your own, you
should not pass here; no, though it were as virtuous to
lie as to live chastely. Therefore go back.

Menenius. Prithee, fellow, remember my name is
Menenius, always factionary on the party of your
30 general.

2 *Watch.* Howsoever you have been his liar, as you
say you have, I am one that, telling true under him,
must say you cannot pass. Therefore go back.

Menenius. Has he dined, canst thou tell? For I would
not speak with him till after dinner.

1 *Watch.* You are a Roman, are you?

Menenius. I am, as thy general is.

1 *Watch.* Then you should hate Rome, as he does.
Can you, when you have pushed out your gates the very

defender of them, and in a violent popular ignorance 40
given your enemy your shield, think to front his
revenges with the easy groans of old women, the
virginal palms of your daughters, or with the palsied
intercession of such a decayed dotant as you seem to be?
Can you think to blow out the intended fire your city is
ready to flame in, with such weak breath as this? No,
you are deceived; therefore, back to Rome, and prepare
for your execution. You are condemned; our general
has sworn you out of reprieve and pardon.

Menenius. Sirrah, if thy captain knew I were here, he 50
would use me with estimation.

2 *Watch.* Come, my captain knows you not.

Menenius. I mean, thy general.

1 *Watch.* My general cares not for you. Back, I say;
go, lest I let forth your half-pint of blood. Back—that's
the utmost of your having. Back.

Menenius. Nay, but, fellow, fellow—

'*Enter CORIOLANUS with AUFIDIUS*'

Coriolanus. What's the matter?

Menenius. Now, you companion, I'll say an errand
for you; you shall know now that I am in estimation; 60
you shall perceive that a Jack guardant cannot office me
from my son Coriolanus. Guess but by my entertainment with him if thou stand'st not i' th' state of hanging,
or of some death more long in spectatorship and crueller
in suffering; behold now presently, and swoon for
what's to come upon thee. [*to Coriolanus*] The glorious
gods sit in hourly synod about thy particular prosperity,
and love thee no worse than thy old father Menenius
does! O my son, my son! thou art preparing fire for us;
look thee, here's water to quench it. I was hardly moved 70
to come to thee; but being assured none but myself

8-2

could move thee, I have been blown out of your gates
with sighs; and conjure thee to pardon Rome and thy
petitionary countrymen. The good gods assuage thy
wrath, and turn the dregs of it upon this varlet here;
this, who, like a block, hath denied my access to thee.

Coriolanus. Away!

Menenius. How! away!

Coriolanus. Wife, mother, child, I know not.
    My affairs

80 Are servanted to others. Though I owe
My revenge properly, my remission lies
In Volscian breasts. That we have been familiar,
Ingrate forgetfulness shall poison rather
Than pity note how much. Therefore be gone.
Mine ears against your suits are stronger than
Your gates against my force. Yet, for I loved thee,
Take this along; I writ it for thy sake,
And would have sent it. [*gives him a letter.*] Another
    word, Menenius,
I will not hear thee speak. [*turns away*] This
    man, Aufidius,

90 Was my beloved in Rome: yet thou behold'st.

Aufidius. You keep a constant temper.

                 [*Coriolanus and Aufidius go*

1 *Watch.* Now, sir, is your name Menenius?

2 *Watch.* 'Tis a spell, you see, of much power. You
know the way home again.

1 *Watch.* Do you hear how we are shent for keeping
your greatness back?

2 *Watch.* What cause, do you think, I have to swoon?

Menenius. I neither care for th' world nor your
general: for such things as you, I can scarce think there's

100 any, you're so slight. He that hath a will to die by himself
fears it not from another. Let your general do his worst.

For you, be that you are, long; and your misery increase
with your age! I say to you, as I was said to, Away!

[*goes*

1 *Watch.* A noble fellow, I warrant him.

2 *Watch.* The worthy fellow is our general: he's the
rock, the oak not to be wind-shaken.   [*they go*

[5. 3.]   *The tent of Coriolanus*

CORIOLANUS *seated before it, in a chair of state with*
AUFIDIUS *and others about him*

Coriolanus. We will before the walls of Rome
          to-morrow
Set down our host. My partner in this action,
You must report to th' Volscian lords how plainly
I have borne this business.
Aufidius.   Only their ends
You have respected; stopped your ears against
The general suit of Rome; never admitted
A private whisper—no, not with such friends
That thought them sure of you.
Coriolanus.   This last old man,
Whom with a cracked heart I have sent to Rome,
Loved me above the measure of a father,   10
Nay, godded me indeed. Their latest refuge
Was to send him; for whose old love I have—
Though I showed sourly to him—once more offered
The first conditions, which they did refuse
And cannot now accept; to grace him only
That thought he could do more, a very little
I have yielded to. Fresh embassies and suits,
Nor from the state nor private friends, hereafter

Will I lend ear to. [*shouting heard*] Ha! what shout
    is this?
20 Shall I be tempted to infringe my vow
In the same time 'tis made? I will not.

    '*Enter*', *in mourning habits*, '*VIRGILIA, VOLUMNIA,
      VALERIA, young MARCIUS, with Attendants*'

My wife comes foremost; then the honoured mould
Wherein this trunk was framed, and in her hand
The grandchild to her blood. But out, affection!
All bond and privilege of nature, break!
Let it be virtuous to be obstinate.
What is that curtsy worth? or those doves' eyes,
Which can make gods forsworn? I melt, and am not
Of stronger earth than others. My mother bows;
30 As if Olympus to a molehill should
In supplication nod: and my young boy
Hath an aspect of intercession which
Great Nature cries 'Deny not.' Let the Volsces
Plough Rome, and harrow Italy: I'll never
Be such a gosling to obey instinct, but stand
As if a man were author of himself
And knew no other kin.
    Virgilia.   My lord and husband!
    Coriolanus. These eyes are not the same I wore
      in Rome.
    Virgilia. The sorrow that delivers us thus changed
40 Makes you think so.
    (*Coriolanus.* [*rising*] Like a dull actor now
I have forgot my part and I am out,
Even to a full disgrace. [*goes to her*] Best of my flesh,
Forgive my tyranny; but do not say,
For that, 'Forgive our Romans.' O, a kiss
Long as my exile, sweet as my revenge!

Now, by the jealous queen of heaven, that kiss
I carried from thee, dear, and my true lip
Hath virgined it e'er since. You gods! I prate,
And the most noble mother of the world
Leave unsaluted. Sink, my knee, i' th' earth;   [*kneels* 50
Of thy deep duty more impression show
Than that of common sons.
   Volumnia.   O, stand up blest!
Whilst with no softer cushion than the flint
I kneel before thee, and unproperly
Show duty, as mistaken all this while
Between the child and parent.   [*kneels*
   Coriolanus.   What's this?
Your knees to me? to your corrected son?
                          [*raises her*
Then let the pebbles on the hungry beach
Fillip the stars; then let the mutinous winds
Strike the proud cedars 'gainst the fiery sun,   60
Murd'ring impossibility, to make
What cannot be, slight work.
   Volumnia.   Thou art my warrior;
I holp to frame thee. Do you know this lady?
   Coriolanus. The noble sister of Publicola,
The moon of Rome, chaste as the icicle
That's curdied by the frost from purest snow
And hangs on Dian's temple—dear Valeria!
   Volumnia. [*showing young Marcius*] This is a poor
        epitome of yours,
Which by th' interpretation of full time
May show like all yourself.
   Coriolanus.   The god of soldiers,   70
With the consent of supreme Jove, inform
Thy thoughts with nobleness, that thou mayst prove
To shame unvulnerable, and stick i' th' wars

Like a great sea-mark, standing every flaw,
And saving those that eye thee!
 Volumnia.   Your knee, sirrah.
 Coriolanus. That's my brave boy!
 Volumnia. Even he, your wife, this lady, and myself
Are suitors to you.
 Coriolanus.   I beseech you, peace!
Or, if you'ld ask, remember this before:
80 The things I have forsworn to grant may never
Be held by you denials. Do not bid me
Dismiss my soldiers, or capitulate
Again with Rome's mechanics. Tell me not
Wherein I seem unnatural; desire not
T' allay my rages and revenges with
Your colder reasons.
 Volumnia.   O, no more, no more!
You have said you will not grant us any thing;
For we have nothing else to ask but that
Which you deny already. Yet we will ask,
90 That, if you fail in our request, the blame
May hang upon your hardness: therefore hear us.
 Coriolanus. Aufidius, and you Volsces, mark;
   for we'll
Hear nought from Rome in private. [*sits*]
   Your request?
 Volumnia. Should we be silent and not speak,
   our raiment
And state of bodies would bewray what life
We have led since thy exile. Think with thyself
How more unfortunate than all living women
Are we come hither; since that thy sight, which should
Make our eyes flow with joy, hearts dance
   with comforts,
100 Constrains them weep and shake with fear and sorrow,

Making the mother, wife, and child, to see
The son, the husband, and the father, tearing
His country's bowels out. And to poor we
Thine enmity's most capital: thou barr'st us
Our prayers to the gods, which is a comfort
That all but we enjoy. For how can we,
Alas, how can we for our country pray,
Whereto we are bound, together with thy victory,
Whereto we are bound? Alack, or we must lose
The country, our dear nurse, or else thy person,   110
Our comfort in the country. We must find
An evident calamity, though we had
Our wish, which side should win; for either thou
Must as a foreign recreant be led
With manacles thorough our streets, or else
Triumphantly tread on thy country's ruin,
And bear the palm for having bravely shed
Thy wife and children's blood. For myself, son,
I purpose not to wait on fortune till
These wars determine: if I can not persuade thee   120
Rather to show a noble grace to both parts
Than seek the end of one, thou shalt no sooner
March to assault thy country than to tread—
Trust to't, thou shalt not—on thy mother's womb,
That brought thee to this world.
  Virgilia.   Ay, and mine,
That brought you forth this boy, to keep your name
Living to time.
  Boy.   A' shall not tread on me;
I'll run away till I am bigger, but then I'll fight.
  Coriolanus. Not of a woman's tenderness to be,
Requires nor child nor woman's face to see.   130
I have sat too long.   [*rising*
  Volumnia.   Nay, go not from us thus.

If it were so that our request did tend
To save the Romans, thereby to destroy
The Volsces whom you serve, you might condemn us,
As poisonous of your honour: no; our suit
Is, that you reconcile them: while the Volsces
May say 'This mercy we have showed,' the Romans,
'This we received;' and each in either side
Give the all-hail to thee, and cry 'Be blest
140 For making up this peace!' Thou know'st, great son,
The end of war's uncertain; but this certain,
That, if thou conquer Rome, the benefit
Which thou shalt thereby reap is such a name
Whose repetition will be dogged with curses;
Whose chronicle thus writ: 'The man was noble,
But with his last attempt he wiped it out,
Destroyed his country, and his name remains
To th' ensuing age abhorred.' Speak to me, son:
Thou hast affected the fine strains of honour,
150 To imitate the graces of the gods;
To tear with thunder the wide cheeks o' th' air,
And yet to charge thy sulphur with a bolt
That should but rive an oak. Why dost not speak?
Think'st thou it honourable for a noble man
Still to remember wrongs? Daughter, speak you:
He cares not for your weeping. Speak thou, boy:
Perhaps thy childishness will move him more
Than can our reasons. There's no man in the world
More bound to 's mother, yet here he lets me prate
160 Like one i' th' stocks. Thou hast never in thy life
Showed thy dear mother any courtesy,
When she, poor hen, fond of no second brood,
Has clucked thee to the wars, and safely home
Loaden with honour. Say my request's unjust,
And spurn me back; but if it be not so,

Thou art not honest, and the gods will plague thee,
That thou restrain'st from me the duty which
To a mother's part belongs. He turns away:
Down, ladies; let us shame him with our knees.
To his surname Coriolanus 'longs more pride   170
Than pity to our prayers. Down: an end;
This is the last: so we will home to Rome,
And die among our neighbours. Nay, behold's!
This boy, that cannot tell what he would have,
But kneels and holds up hands for fellowship,
Does reason our petition with more strength
Than thou hast to deny 't. Come, let us go:
This fellow had a Volscian to his mother;
His wife is in Corioli, and his child
Like him by chance. Yet give us our dispatch.   180
I am hushed until our city be a-fire,   [*he turns*
And then I'll speak a little.

'*Holds her by the hand, silent*'

Coriolanus.   O mother, mother!
What have you done? Behold, the heavens do ope,
The gods look down, and this unnatural scene
They laugh at. O my mother, mother! O!
You have won a happy victory to Rome;
But, for your son—believe it, O, believe it—
Most dangerously you have with him prevailed,
If not most mortal to him. But let it come.
Aufidius, though I cannot make true wars,   190
I'll frame convenient peace. Now, good Aufidius,
Were you in my stead, would you have heard
A mother less? or granted less, Aufidius?
  Aufidius. I was moved withal.
  Coriolanus.   I dare be sworn you were!
And, sir, it is no little thing to make

Mine eyes to sweat compassion. But, good sir,
What peace you'll make, advise me: for my part,
I'll not to Rome, I'll back with you; and pray you
Stand to me in this cause. O mother! wife!

       [*speaks with them apart*

200 (*Aufidius.* I am glad thou hast set thy mercy and
    thy honour
At difference in thee. Out of that I'll work
Myself a former fortune.

 Coriolanus. [*coming forward with Volumnia and*
    Virgilia] Ay, by and by;
But we will drink together; and you shall bear
A better witness back than words, which we
On like conditions will have counter-sealed.
Come, enter with us. Ladies, you deserve
To have a temple built you. All the swords
In Italy, and her confederate arms,
Could not have made this peace.

         [*they enter the tent*

[5. 4.] *Rome. A street not far from the gate*

   '*Enter* MENENIUS *and* SICINIUS'

 Menenius. See you yond coign o' th' Capitol, yond
cornerstone?

 Sicinius. Why, what of that?

 Menenius. If it be possible for you to displace it with
your little finger, there is some hope the ladies of Rome,
especially his mother, may prevail with him. But I say
there is no hope in't: our throats are sentenced, and stay
upon execution.

 Sicinius. Is't possible that so short a time can alter the
10 condition of a man?

Menenius. There is difference between a grub and a butterfly; yet your butterfly was a grub. This Marcius is grown from man to dragon: he has wings; he's more than a creeping thing.

Sicinius. He loved his mother dearly.

Menenius. So did he me: and he no more remembers his mother now than an eight-year-old horse. The tartness of his face sours ripe grapes; when he walks, he moves like an engine and the ground shrinks before his 20 treading. He is able to pierce a corslet with his eye, talks like a knell, and his hum is a battery. He sits in his state as a thing made for Alexander. What he bids be done is finished with his bidding. He wants nothing of a god but eternity and a heaven to throne in.

Sicinius. Yes, mercy, if you report him truly.

Menenius. I paint him in the character. Mark what mercy his mother shall bring from him: there is no more mercy in him than there is milk in a male tiger; that shall our poor city find. And all this is 'long of you.

Sicinius. The gods be good unto us!   30

Menenius. No, in such a case the gods will not be good unto us. When we banished him, we respected not them; and, he returning to break our necks, they respect not us.

'*Enter a Messenger*'

Messenger. Sir, if you'ld save your life, fly to
          your house:
The plebeians have got your fellow-tribune,
And hale him up and down; all swearing if
The Roman ladies bring not comfort home
They'll give him death by inches.

'*Enter another Messenger*'

Sicinius.   What's the news?

40   2 *Messenger*. Good news, good news! The ladies
       have prevailed,
The Volscians are dislodged, and Marcius gone.
A merrier day did never yet greet Rome,
No, not th' expulsion of the Tarquins.
   Sicinius.   Friend,
Art thou certain this is true? Is't most certain?
   2 *Messenger*. As certain as I know the sun is fire.
Where have you lurked, that you make doubt of it?
Ne'er through an arch so hurried the blown tide,
As the recomforted through the gates. Why, hark you!

   '*Trumpets, hautboys, drums, beat, all together*'

The trumpets, sackbuts, psalteries, and fifes,
50 Tabors and cymbals, and the shouting Romans,
Make the sun dance. ['*a shout*'] Hark you!
   Menenius.   This is good news.
I will go meet the ladies. This Volumnia
Is worth of consuls, senators, patricians,
A city full; of tribunes such as you,
A sea and land full. You have prayed well to-day:
This morning for ten thousand of your throats
I'ld not have given a doit. [*shouts, trumpets, etc. heard
     louder*] Hark, how they joy!
Sicinius. First, the gods bless you for your tidings; next,
Accept my thankfulness.
   2 *Messenger*.   Sir, we have all
60 Great cause to give great thanks.
   Sicinius.   They are near the city!
   2 *Messenger*. Almost at point to enter.
   Sicinius.   We will meet them,
And help the joy.   [*they go towards the gate*

[5. 5.] *Enter in procession the Ladies with a great press*
of Senators, Patricians and People

1 *Senator.* Behold our patroness, the life of Rome!
Call all your tribes together, praise the gods,
And make triumphant fires; strew flowers before them.
Unshout the noise that banished Marcius,
Repeal him with the welcome of his mother;
Cry 'Welcome, ladies, welcome!'
　All.　　　　　　　　　Welcome, ladies,
Welcome!
　　　[*they pass on; 'a flourish with drums and trumpets'*

[5. 6.]　　　*Corioli. A public place*
'*Enter TULLUS AUFIDIUS, with Attendants*'

Aufidius. Go tell the lords o' th' city I am here:
Deliver them this paper: having read it,
Bid them repair to th' market-place, where I,
Even in theirs and in the commons' ears,
Will vouch the truth of it. Him I accuse
The city ports by this hath entered, and
Intends t' appear before the people, hoping
To purge himself with words. Dispatch.
　　　　　　　　　　　　　　[*Attendants go*

'*Enter three or four Conspirators of AUFIDIUS' faction*'

Most welcome!
　1 *Conspirator.* How is it with our general?
　Aufidius.　　　　　　　　　Even so　　10
As with a man by his own alms empoisoned,
And with his charity slain.
　2 *Conspirator.*　　　　　Most noble sir,

If you do hold the same intent wherein
You wished us parties, we'll deliver you
Of your great danger.

Aufidius.   Sir, I cannot tell;
We must proceed as we do find the people.

3 *Conspirator.* The people will remain uncertain whilst
'Twixt you there's difference; but the fall of either
Makes the survivor heir of all.

Aufidius.   I know it,
20 And my pretext to strike at him admits
A good construction. I raised him, and I pawned
Mine honour for his truth; who being so heightened,
He watered his new plants with dews of flattery,
Seducing so my friends; and, to this end,
He bowed his nature, never known before
But to be rough, unswayable, and free.

3 *Conspirator.* Sir, his stoutness
When he did stand for consul, which he lost
By lack of stooping—

Aufidius.   That I would have spoke of.
30 Being banished for't, he came unto my hearth;
Presented to my knife his throat: I took him,
Made him joint-servant with me; gave him way
In all his own desires; nay, let him choose
Out of my files, his projects to accomplish,
My best and freshest men; served his designments
In mine own person; holp to reap the fame
Which he did end all his; and took some pride
To do myself this wrong: till at the last
I seemed his follower, not partner; and
40 He waged me with his countenance, as if
I had been mercenary.

1 *Conspirator.*   So he did, my lord:
The army marvelled at it; and, in the last,

When he had carried Rome and that we looked
For no less spoil than glory—
Aufidius.   There was it;
For which my sinews shall be stretched upon him.
At a few drops of women's rheum, which are
As cheap as lies, he sold the blood and labour
Of our great action: therefore shall he die,
And I'll renew me in his fall. But hark!

'*Drums and trumpets sound, with great shouts
                of the people*'

 1 *Conspirator.* Your native town you entered like   50
            a post,
And had no welcomes home; but he returns,
Splitting the air with noise.
 1 *Conspirator.*   And patient fools,
Whose children he hath slain, their base throats tear
With giving him glory.
 3 *Conspirator.*   Therefore, at your vantage,
Ere he express himself or move the people
With what he would say, let him feel your sword,
Which we will second. When he lies along,
After your way his tale pronounced shall bury
His reasons with his body.
Aufidius.   Say no more:
Here come the lords.   60

'*Enter the Lords of the city*'

Lords. You are most welcome home.
Aufidius.   I have not deserved it.
But, worthy lords, have you with heed perused
What I have written to you?
Lords.   We have.
 1 *Lord.*   And grieve to hear 't.

9   PSC

What faults he made before the last, I think
Might have found easy fines; but there to end
Where he was to begin, and give away
The benefit of our levies, answering us
With our own charge, making a treaty where
There was a yielding—this admits no excuse.

70 *Aufidius.* He approaches: you shall hear him.

'*Enter* CORIOLANUS, *marching with drum and colours;
the commoners being with him*'

Coriolanus. Hail, lords! I am returned your soldier;
No more infected with my country's love
Than when I parted hence, but still subsisting
Under your great command. You are to know
That prosperously I have attempted, and
With bloody passage led your wars even to
The gates of Rome. Our spoils we have brought home
Doth more than counterpoise a full third part
The charges of the action. We have made peace
80 With no less honour to the Antiates
Than shame to th' Romans; and we here deliver,
Subscribed by th' consuls and patricians,
Together with the seal o' th' senate, what
We have compounded on.

    Aufidius.   Read it not, noble lords;
But tell the traitor in the highest degree
He hath abused your powers.

    Coriolanus. Traitor! how now!

    Aufidius.   Ay, traitor, Marcius!

    Coriolanus.   Marcius!

    Aufidius. Ay, Marcius, Caius Marcius! Dost
       thou think
I'll grace thee with that robbery, thy stol'n name
90 Coriolanus, in Corioli?

You lords and heads o' th' state, perfidiously
He has betrayed your business and given up,
For certain drops of salt, your city Rome,
I say 'your city', to his wife and mother;
Breaking his oath and resolution, like
A twist of rotten silk; never admitting
Counsel o' th' war; but at his nurse's tears
He whined and roared away your victory;
That pages blushed at him and men of heart
Looked wond'ring each at other.
    Coriolanus.   Hear'st thou, Mars? 100
    Aufidius. Name not the god, thou boy of tears!
    Coriolanus.   Ha!
    Aufidius. No more.
    Coriolanus. Measureless liar, thou hast made
         my heart
Too great for what contains it. 'Boy!' O slave!
Pardon me, lords, 'tis the first time that ever
I was forced to scold. Your judgements, my
         grave lords,
Must give this cur the lie: and his own notion—
Who wears my stripes impressed upon him; that
Must bear my beating to his grave—shall join
To thrust the lie unto him.   110
    1 *Lord*. Peace, both, and hear me speak.
    Coriolanus. Cut me to pieces, Volsces; men
         and lads,
Stain all your edges on me. 'Boy'! False hound!
If you have writ your annals true, 'tis there,
That, like an eagle in a dove-cote, I
Fluttered your Volscians in Corioli.
Alone I did it. 'Boy!'
    Aufidius.   Why, noble lords,
Will you be put in mind of his blind fortune,

Which was your shame, by this unholy braggart,
120 Fore your own eyes and ears?
   The Conspirators.   Let him die for't.
   The People. 'Tear him to pieces.' 'Do it presently.'
'He killed my son.' 'My daughter.' 'He killed my
cousin Marcus.' 'He killed my father.'
   2 *Lord.* Peace, ho! no outrage: peace!
The man is noble, and his fame folds-in
This orb o' th' earth. His last offences to us
Shall have judicious hearing. Stand, Aufidius,
And trouble not the peace.
   Coriolanus.   O that I had him,
With six Aufidiuses or more—his tribe,
130 To use my lawful sword!
   Aufidius.   Insolent villain!
   The conspirators. Kill, kill, kill, kill, kill him!

    The Conspirators draw, and kill Coriolanus:
        Aufidius stands on his body

   Lords.   Hold, hold, hold, hold!
   Aufidius. My noble masters, hear me speak.
   1 *Lord.*   O Tullus!
   2 *Lord.* Thou hast done a deed whereat valour
      will weep.
   3 *Lord.* Tread not upon him. Masters all, be quiet;
Put up your swords.
   Aufidius. My lords, when you shall know—as in
      this rage
Provoked by him, you cannot—the great danger
Which this man's life did owe you, you'll rejoice
That he is thus cut off. Please it your honours
140 To call me to your senate, I'll deliver
Myself your loyal servant, or endure
Your heaviest censure.

1 *Lord.*   Bear from hence his body,
And mourn you for him. Let him be regarded
As the most noble corse that ever herald
Did follow to his urn.

2 *Lord.*   His own impatience
Takes from Aufidius a great part of blame.
Let's make the best of it.

Aufidius.   My rage is gone,
And I am struck with sorrow. Take him up:
Help, three o' th' chiefest soldiers; I'll be one.
Beat thou the drum, that it speak mournfully: 150
Trail your steel pikes. Though in this city he
Hath widowed and unchilded many a one,
Which to this hour bewail the injury,
Yet he shall have a noble memory.
Assist.

['*exeunt bearing away the body of Coriolanus;
a dead march sounded*']

ALONG, prostrate on the ground, at full length; 5. 6. 57

AMAZONIAN, as beardless as those of the Amazons (women warriors of Greek legend); 2. 2. 89

AN, if; 2. 1. 128, etc.

ANCUS MARCIUS, legendary king of Rome, the third after Romulus; 2. 3. 238

AN-HUNGRY, hungry (here only Sh.); 1. 1. 204

ANON, in a short while; 2. 3. 140, 143, etc.

ANSWER (sb.), reply to, or defence in, a charge; 3. 1. 176

ANSWER (vb.), (i) meet in combat; 1. 2. 19; 1. 4. 53; (ii) act in conformity with, 'play up to' (E. K. Chambers); 2. 3. 258; (iii) suffer the consequences, pay the penalty; 3. 1. 162; (iv) stand on one's defence; 3. 1. 323; (v) repay, requite; 5. 6. 67

ANTIATES, people of Antium (3. 1. 11), a town in Latium, chief city of the Volsces; 1. 6. 53, etc.

ANTIQUE, old-fashioned (cf. M.N.D. 5. 1. 3), out of date; 2. 3. 118

ANVIL, fig., body (upon which the sword of an enemy strikes); 4. 5. 113

APPREHENSION, perception; 2. 3. 223

APPROBATION, (i) 'prosperous approbation' = 'confirmed success'; 2. 1. 102; (ii) approval, ratification; 2. 3. 143, 250

APPROVE, approve of; 3. 2. 8

APRON-MAN, mechanic (wearing a leather apron); 4. 6. 97

APT, impressionable, yielding; 3. 2. 29

APTNESS, readiness; 4. 3. 23

ARMS, army, armed forces; 5. 3. 208

ARRIVE, reach, arrive at; 2. 3. 180

ARTICLE, stipulation; 2. 3. 195

ARTICULATE, come to terms; 1. 9. 77

AS, as if; 1. 1. 212; 5. 1. 64

ASH, spear of ash wood; 4. 5. 111

ASPECT, look, appearance; 5. 3. 32

ATONE, become reconciled; 4. 6. 73

ATTACH, arrest; 3. 1. 174

ATTEND, (i) ('attend upon'), accompany; 1. 1. 236; (ii) await, wait for; 1. 1. 75, 244; 1. 10. 30; 2. 2. 158; 3. 1. 330; 3. 2. 138; (iii) listen; 1. 9. 4

AUDIBLE, quick of hearing (O.E.D. 2); 4. 5. 229

AUDIENCE, (i) attention, silence; 3. 3. 40; (ii) formal interview; 2. 1. 71

AUDIT, statement of accounts; 1. 1. 143

AUGER, tool for boring small holes (cf. Macb. 2. 3. 122); 4. 6. 88

AUGURER, augur, member of Roman priestly college whose business was to study auguries and decide whether favourable or unfavourable to an undertaking; 2. 1. 1

AVOID, quit; 4. 5. 24, 33

BALD, (i) (*a*) mod. sense, (*b*) paltry; 3. 1. 164; (ii) bare-headed; 4. 5. 200

BALE, injury; 'have b.', get the worst of it; 1. 1. 162

BARE, mere, with no word of restitution; 5. 1. 20

BASTARD, i.e. spurious; 3. 2. 56

BAT, stick, club; 1. 1. 55, 160

BATTEN, grow fat; 4. 5. 34

BATTLE, army; 1. 6. 51

BE, (i) 'be in', be involved in (cf. *L.L.L.* 4. 3. 18 'if the other three were in'; O.E.D. 'in' adv. 6*b*); 3. 2. 64; (ii) 'be off', doff the cap; 2. 3. 99; (iii) 'be with', comply with (their wish), lit. 'go along' with (cf. O.E.D. 'with' 20, 21*a*); 3. 2. 74

BEAM, lit. ray of light; here, fig.=range of vision; 3. 2. 5

BEAR, (i) conduct, manage, carry on; 1. 1. 269; 1. 6. 82; 4. 7. 21; 5. 3. 4; (ii) be endowed with; 2. 3. 179; (iii) carry; 3. 1. 212; (iv) endure; 1. 1. 99; 3. 1. 249; 3. 2. 35; 3. 3. 33

BEASTLY, like cattle; 2. 1. 93

*BEGNAW, gnaw, rot; 2. 1. 183

BELONGING. Either (sb.) accessory; hence, here=trappings, caparison. Or (adj.) appertaining; 1. 9. 62

BENCH, seat of authority, court, government (cf. *Tim.* 4. 1. 5); 3. 1. 106, 167

BENCHER, member of the senate, senator; 2. 1. 80

BEWITCHMENT, enchanting manner; 2. 3. 100

BEWRAY, reveal; 5. 3. 95

BILLET (vb.), enroll; enter on a list; 4. 3. 45

BISSON, purblind; 2. 1. 63

BLANK, a blank ticket in a lottery; 5. 2. 10

BLEEDING, fig. unhealed, unsettled; 2. 1. 75

BLESS, guard, protect; 1. 3. 46

BLESSED, 'blessed to do', mod. 'happy to do'; 2. 2. 56

BLOCK, lit. a lump of wood or stone; here (*a*) blockhead, (*b*) 'a lump of wood...that obstructs one's way; fig. an obstacle or obstruction' (O.E.D. 11); 5. 2. 76

BLOOD, 'in bl.' (fig. from the chase, of a hound) in full vigour; 4. 5. 217; hence, 'worst in bl.'=in worst condition for running; 1. 1. 158

BLOODY, blood-red, 'bl. flag', a sign of warfare; 2. 1. 74

BLOWN=either 'swollen' or 'wind-driven'; 5. 4. 47

BODY OF THE WEAL, commonwealth, body corporate; 2. 3. 180

BOLTED, lit. (of flour) passed through a sieve or bolting-cloth so as to separate the flour from the bran, i.e. to rid it of its coarser elements, thus fig. refined, carefully sifted; 3. 1. 320

BONNET (vb.), take off bonnet or cap as a sign of respect (cf. Cotgrave, 1611, '*bonneter*, to put off one's cap unto'; and the mod. coll. 'to cap someone'); 2. 2. 25–6

BORE, small hole; 4. 6. 88

Bosom, (a) 'the seat of emotions, desires, etc.' (O.E.D. 6b), the 'heart' (cf. Macb. 5. 3. 44), (b) phys. 'the cavity of the stomach' (O.E.D. 4b); 3. 1. 131; 3. 2. 57

Botcher, cobbler, or mender of old clothes; 2. 1. 86

Bottom, essence (O.E.D. 12); 4. 5. 203

Bound (ppl. of obs. 'boun'=to prepare, set out, to go), 'bound to'=setting out for; 3. 1. 54

Bound (ppl. of 'bind'), under an obligation; 5. 3. 108, 109, 159

Bountiful, bountifully; 2. 3. 101

Brand, (i) stigma; 3. 1. 302; (ii) torch; 4. 6. 116

Brave, (i) fine; 2. 2. 5; (ii) (of conduct) insolent; 4. 5. 17

Brawn, arm; 4. 5. 123

Break, fall out, quarrel; 4. 6. 49

Breath, voice, speech (O.E.D. 9); 2. 2. 148

Breathe, pause, 'rest from action' (Schmidt). Cf. 1 H. IV, 1. 3. 110, 'three times they breathed'; 1. 6. 1

Briefly, 'within a short time, measured either backwards or forwards' (O.E.D. 2); 1. 6. 16

Broil, uproarious strife; 3. 1. 33

Bruising, lit. crushing; hence here, fig. damaging, injurious; 2. 3. 201

Budge, flinch; 1. 6. 44

Budger, one who flinches; 1. 8. 5

Bulk, flat projecting framework in front of shop (cf.

Oth. 5. 1. 1). 'Butchers and fishmongers displayed their goods on them; tailors and cobblers sat and worked on them' (G.G.); 2. 1. 207

Buss, kiss; 3. 2. 75

Call up, rouse in any way; 2. 3. 193

Cankered, depraved, corrupt; 4. 5. 94

Canon, law (properly, Church law); 3. 1. 90

Canopy, fig. firmament; 4. 5. 40

Cap, doffing of the cap; fig. bow; 2. 1. 67

Capital, deadly, fatal; 5. 3. 104

Capitol, senate-house (cf. Titus and Caes.), properly the Capitoline Hill N.W. of the Forum, near which in the Curia Hostilia the Senate generally met; 1. 1. 47, 191, etc.

Capitulate, 'arrange or propose terms, bargain, parley'; 5. 3. 82

Carbonado (<Sp. carbonada, 'a Carbonado on the coles' (Minshen)), meat scored or 'scotched' across and broiled; 4. 5. 193

Cares, solicitude for others; 3. 1. 137

Carry, (i) win; 2. 1. 235; 4. 7. 27; 5. 6. 43; (ii) 'c. it', win; 2. 2. 4; 2. 3. 36

Casque, helmet (as symbol of the warrior's life); 4. 7. 43

Cast, (i) 'cast upon', confer on; 2. 1. 199; (ii) throw up; 4. 6. 131

Cat. A term of contempt (cf. All's, 4. 3. 234); 4. 2. 34

Cato, the elder Cato, 234–
149 B.C., famous after the
3rd Punic War for his
'delenda est Carthago'; 1. 4.
57

Cause, (i) case to be tried in a
court of law; 3. 3. 18;
(ii) disease, ailment (<late
Lat. 'causa'); 3. 1. 234

Cautelous, crafty (cf. *Caes.*
2. 1. 129); 4. 1. 33

Censorinus, Martius C., of
the same family as Corio-
lanus, but not ancestor,
censor *c.* 265 B.C.; 2. 3. 242

Censure, (i) opinion;
1. 1. 267; (ii) condemna-
tion; 3. 3. 46

Censure (vb.), judge, estimate;
2. 1. 22, 24

Centurion, commander of a
century (*q.v.*); 4. 3. 44

Century, a division of the
Roman army, originally of
100 men; 1. 7. 3

Change of honours (sb.), a
new or fresh set (gen. of
clothes); 2. 1. 195

Changeling, a fickle person
(cf. *1 H. IV*, 5. 1. 76);
4. 7. 11

Charge (sb.), body of troops
under command; 4. 3. 45

Charge (vb.), (i) blame, accuse; 3. 3. 42; (ii) adjure,
entreat earnestly (cf.
Schmidt); 4. 6. 113

Charm, magic spell; 1. 5. 22

Charter, lit. a document in
which a king grants a privilege; and so, privilege,
conceded right; 1. 9. 14;
2. 3. 179

Chat (vb.), gossip about; 2. 1.
205

Choir (vb.), make music
(with); 3. 2. 113

Circumvention, means or
power to circumvent; 1. 2. 6

Clap to, shut (a door)
smartly; 1. 4. 52

Clip, embrace; 1. 6. 29; 4. 5.
112

Cluster, mob; 4. 6. 123, 129

Cobbled, (of shoes) patched,
clumsily or ill-mended; 1. 1.
195

Cockle, darnel, tares, *Lolium
temulentum.* A.V. Matth.
xiii. 25. Rheims New Test.
(1582) reads 'cockle' for
'tares'. The mod. 'corn-
cockle' is a different plant;
3. 1. 70

Cog, wheedle; 3. 2. 133

Coign, corner-stone, (in mod.
sp.) quoin; 5. 4. 1

Cold, (i) cool, unimpassioned;
3. 1. 219; (ii) without power
to influence (cf. *M.V.* 2. 7.
73); 5. 3. 86

Come, (i) interj. expressing
mild rebuke; 1. 1. 271; (ii)
'c. off'=get clear, with-
draw successfully (from a
battle) (cf. *H. V*, 3. 6. 71);
1. 6. 1; 2. 2. 110

Comely, becoming, decorous;
4. 6. 27

Comfort, happiness, cheerful-
ness; 5. 3. 99

Comfortable, cheerful; 1. 3. 2

Command, (i) body of troops
under command of officer;
1. 6. 84; (ii) air of command,
of authority; 4. 5. 64

Commanded (mil.), to be c.
under=to be under the
command of (cf. O.E.D.
'commanded'); 1. 1. 261

COMMISSION, (i) military warrant for an officer; 1. 2. 26; 1. 7. 14; (ii) troops assigned to an officer by warrant, military command; 4. 5. 14

COMMON (adj.), (i) of the common people; 2. 2. 51; 3. 1. 22; (ii) 'be common', make oneself cheap or not sufficiently exclusive (cf. *Son.* 69. 14); 2. 3. 94

COMMON (sb.) (i) common people; 1. 1. 150; 3. 1. 29; (ii) what is usual; 4. 1. 32

COMMONALTY, common people; 1. 1. 28

COMMONERS, common people, plebians; 2. 1. 224

COMPANION, term of contempt, 'fellow'; 4. 5. 13; 5. 2. 59

COMPLEXION, lit. blend of humours which determined mental and bodily temperament; hence, temperament, disposition, 'nature'; 2. 1. 209

COMPOSITION, agreement or 'compromise'; 3. 1. 3

COMPOUND, agree, come to terms, settle by concession; 5. 6. 84

CON, get to know, commit to memory, learn by heart; 4. 1. 11

CONCLUDE, come to a decision, decide; 3. 1. 145

CONDEMNED, damnable; 1. 8. 15

CONDITION, (i) terms of agreement; 1. 10. 2, 3; (ii) (*a*) terms, (*b*) character, quality; 1. 10. 5, 6; 5. 4. 10; (iii) behaviour, manner; 2. 3. 96

CONFIRMED, (i) resolute, determined; 1. 3. 61; (ii) confirmed in office; 2. 3. 208

CONFOUND, waste, consume; 1. 6. 17

CONFUSION, anarchy, destruction (civil); 3. 1. 110, 189; 4. 6. 29

CONJURE, adjure, beseech, implore; 5. 2. 73

CONSPECTUITY, power of sight ('app. a humorous or random formation from "conspectus"', O.E.D.); 2. 1. 63

CONSTANT, unshaken in purpose or promise (cf. *Caes.* 3. 1. 60); 1. 1. 238; 5. 2. 91

CONTENT, agreed, 'all right'; 2. 3. 46

CONTRIVE, plot; 3. 3. 63

CONVENIENT, appropriate, suitable; 1. 5. 12; 5. 3. 191

CONVENT (vb.), convene; 2. 2. 52

CONVERSE (with), be conversant with, associate (freq.); 2. 1. 50

CONVERSATION, intercourse, society; 2. 1. 92

CONVEYANCE, channel (for conveying a liquid); 5. 1. 54

CONY, rabbit; 4. 5. 218

CORMORANT (adj.), insatiably greedy; 1. 1. 120

COUNTENANCE, favour, patronage; 5. 6. 40

COUNTERFEITLY, feigningly; 2. 3. 99

COUNTERPOISE (vb.), balance in quality, equal in value; 2. 2. 85

COUNTER-SEALED, sealed by both parties; 5. 3. 205

COURAGE, spirit, disposition; 3. 3. 92

COURSE, one of a succession or series; 1. 5. 16

COVERTURE, covering for the body, apparel, clothing; 1. 9. 46

COXCOMB, head (ludicrous or jeering); 4. 6. 135

COY (vb.), disdain; 5. 1. 6

CRACK, pert little boy, little imp (cf. *2 H. IV*, 3. 2. 32); 1. 3. 69

CRAFT (vb.), (*a*) carry out a job, (*b*) act craftily; 4. 6. 119

CRANK (sb.), winding passage; 1. 1. 136

CROOKED, wry; 2. 1. 55

CRY (sb.), pack (of hounds); 3. 3. 120; 4. 6. 148

CRY HAVOC, *v.* Havoc; 3. 1. 273

CUNNING, knowledge (of life), skill (in living), i.e. philosophy; 4. 1. 9

CUPBOARD (vb.), hoard up; 1. 1. 99

CURDIED, congealed; poss. 'curdled' misprinted; 5. 3. 66

CUSHION, (i) seat (in Senate); 3. 1. 101; (ii) seat (as symbol of peaceful life of ease and civil authority); 4. 7. 43

DAMASK, orig. colour of Damascus rose, here, red; 2. 1. 213

DARKEN, deprive of lustre (cf. *Ant.* 3. 1. 24), or eclipse; 4. 7. 5

DAW, jackdaw, type of extreme stupidity; 4. 5. 46

DEADLY, mod. slang 'like sin'; 2. 1. 60

DEAR, valuable, precious; 1. 1. 19; 1. 6. 72

DEARTH, famine; lit. dearness, scarcity (e.g. of corn); 1. 1. 66

DEBILE, weak, feeble; 1. 9. 48

DECLINE (vb.), fall; 2. 1. 159

DEED-ACHIEVING, achieved by deeds; 2. 1. 171

DEGREE, step; 2. 2. 24

*DEJECTITUDE. A made word < 'dejected', downcast, crestfallen; 4. 5. 214

DELIVER, (i) release (mod. sense); 5. 6. 14; (ii) intr., speak, tell one's tale; 1. 1. 94; (iii) tr. report; 2. 1. 56; 4. 6. 64; (iv) present (cf. *Tw. Nt.* 1. 2. 43); 5. 3. 39; 5. 6. 140

DEMERIT, merit, desert (the orig. sense; cf. *Oth.* 1. 2. 22); 1. 1. 271

DENIAL, refusal; 5. 3. 81

DENY, refuse, reject; 1. 6. 65; 2. 3. 2, 205, 208, 209; 5. 2. 76; 5. 3. 33, 89, 177

DESERVED, deserving (cf. *All's*, 2. 1. 189); 3. 1. 290

DESIGNMENT, undertaking, enterprise (cf. *Oth.* 2. 1. 22); 5. 6. 35

DESPITE, contempt; 3. 1. 163; 3. 3. 139

DETERMINE, (i) decide; 2. 2. 35; 4. 1. 35; (ii) come to an end, terminate; 3. 3. 43; 5. 3. 120

DEUCALION, Prometheus' son, who, warned by his father, escaped with his wife Pyrrha the world-wide deluge like the biblical Noah by building a boat wh. landed on Parnassus as Noah's ark on Ararat when the flood subsided; 2. 1. 89

DIAN, Diana, goddess of chastity; 5. 3. 67

DIET, lit. prescribe a diet, hence (i) fatten, inflate;

1. 9. 52; (ii) bring into condition, i.e. render amiable by a good dinner; 5. 1. 57

DIFFERENCE, (i) variance; 5. 3. 201; (ii) disagreement; 5. 6. 18

DIFFERENCY, difference (in mod. sense); 5. 4. 11

DIGEST, (a) mod. sense, (b) interpret, understand; 1. 1. 149; 3. 1. 131

DIRECTLY, face to face; 1. 6. 58; 4. 5. 191 (or plainly, unambiguously)

DISBENCH, cause to leave seat, unseat (usu. of Inn's of Court membership; only inst. in O.E.D. of general sense); 2. 2. 69

DISCIPLINE (vb.), punish by thrashing; 2. 1. 124

DISCOVER, reveal; 2. 2. 19

DISEASE (vb.), disturb, make uneasy; 1. 3. 106

DISGRACE, misfortune, lit. the disfavour of Fortune (v. O.E.D. 2); 1. 1. 93

DISHONOURED, dishonourable; 3. 1. 60

DISLODGE. A tech. mil. term = 'leave a place of encampment' (O.E.D.); 5. 4. 41

DISPATCH (sb.), (i) execution of a matter; 1. 1. 276; (ii) dismissal, leave to go; 5. 3. 180

DISPATCH (vb.), hasten; 5. 6. 8

DISPOSE OF, make the best of; 4. 7. 40

DISPOSED, inclined; 3. 2. 22

DISPOSITION, inclination, humour; 1. 6. 74; 2. 1. 30; 3. 2. 21

DISPROPERTY (vb.), 'alienate', 'dispossess' (O.E.D.; On.) Better, I think, 'deprive of its essential property', 'reduce to a farce'; 2. 1. 245

DISSEMBLE WITH, disguise, act or speak in contradiction of; 3. 2. 62

DISSOLVED, dispersed; 1. 1. 203

DISTINCTLY, separately; 4. 3. 45

DISTRIBUTE, administer; 3. 3. 99

DIVIDE, share; 1. 6. 87

DOIT, old Dutch coin, worth a $\frac{1}{2}$d. or $\frac{1}{4}$d.; 1. 5. 6; 4. 4. 17; 5. 4. 57

DOTANT, dotard (only known inst.); 5. 2. 44

DOUBLED, redoubled; 2. 2. 114

DOUBT (vb.), fear; 3. 1. 152

DOWNRIGHT (adv.), absolutely; 2. 3. 158

DRACHMA, ancient Greek silver coin, worth c. $9\frac{3}{4}$d. in prewar money; 1. 5. 5

DRAW, gather, assemble; 2. 3. 252

DRAW OUT. Mil. = 'detach from the main body' (O.E.D.), pick out; 1. 6. 84

DRENCH (orig. = drink), 'draught or dose of medicine administered to an animal' (O.E.D.); 2. 1. 116

DULL, stupid (or 'gloomy'); 1. 9. 6

DUTY, reverence; 5. 3. 51, 55, 167

EACH, every; 3. 1. 49

EARTH, substance of which man is made, the human body (cf. Gen. ii. 7; *Rom.* 2. 1. 2, 'turn back, dull earth'); 5. 3. 29

Tree

EASY, requiring little effort; 5. 2. 42

EDGE, sword; 1. 4. 29; 5. 6. 113

EFFECT (vb.), give effect to (*Troil.* 5. 10. 6); 1. 9. 18

ELDER, senator; 1. 1. 225; 2. 2. 40

ELECTION, choice; 2. 3. 218, 228, 254

ELEMENTS, the powers of the air, e.g. 'rain, wind, thunder, fire' (*Lr.* 3. 1. 4); 1. 10. 10

EMBARQUEMENT (of), lit. placing of embargo on ships in port (O.E.D.; cf. also Cotgrave, 1611 'embarquement'), stoppage, bottling up; 1. 10. 23

EMPIRICUTIC (adj.), lit. empirical, (hence) quackery. A 'nonce-word', perh. Sh. coinage; 2. 1. 115

EMULATION, rivalry (or perhaps 'malicious triumph'); 1. 1. 213; 1. 10. 12

END, 'for an end' = in conclusion, to cut the matter short; 2. 1. 241

END (vb.), gather in a crop. 'A dial. variant or corruption [not here textual] of *inn*' (O.E.D.); cf. *All's Well*, 1. 3. 44, 'to in the crop', and *L'Allegro*, 109, 'the corn That ten day labourers could not end'; 5. 6. 37

ENDUE, endow; 2. 3. 138

ENFORCE, (i) lay stress on; 2. 3. 218; so, (ii) 'enforce him with', ply him hard with; 3. 3. 3; (iii) press for, demand; 3. 3. 21

ENGINE, war machine; 5. 4. 20

ENORMITY, irregular conduct, 'deviation from moral rectitude'; 2. 1. 16

ENTERED (in), let in to the secret of; 1. 2. 2

ENTERTAINMENT, (i) 'in the entertainment' = being paid; 4. 3. 45; (ii) welcome, reception; 4. 5. 9; 5. 2. 62

ENVY (sb.), enmity, hate; 1. 8. 4 (or perh. vb. here); 3. 3. 3; 4. 5. 77, 106

ENVY (vb.), feel ill will to; 3. 3. 57; 'envy against' = show malice towards (On.); 3. 3. 95

EPITOME, (*a*) representation in miniature, (*b*) summary or abstract of a speech to be spoken; 5. 3. 68

ESTATE, property, fortune; 2. 1. 112

ESTIMATE, repute, reputation; 3. 3. 114

ESTIMATION, (i) estimate, valuation; 2. 1. 88; (ii) esteem; 2. 2. 27; 2. 3. 96; 5. 2. 51, 60

EVEN (adv.), steadily, without losing one's balance; 4. 7. 37

EVENT, outcome; 2. 1. 267

EVIDENT, indubitable, certain; 4. 7. 52; 5. 3. 112

EXTREMITY, the utmost point (of danger); 3. 2. 41; 4. 1. 4

FABRIC, (i) building; 3. 1. 246; (ii) frame, body; 1. 1. 118

FACTIONARY, active as a partisan (O.E.D.); 5. 2. 29

FAIR (adj.), (i) clean; 1. 9. 69; (ii) even, smooth (mod.

slang 'decent'); 3. 1. 241; (iii) civil, courteous; 3. 2. 96; (iv) fine (iron.); 4. 6. 89

FAIR (adv.), civilly, courteously; 3. 1. 262; 3. 2. 70

FAIRNESS, 'to the fairness of my power'=as becomingly as I can (cf. 'fairly', *M.V.* 1. 1. 128); 1. 9. 73

FAITH. Ellipt. for 'in faith', truly; 2. 2. 7, etc.

FAMILIAR (adj.), intimate; 5. 2. 82

FAMOUSLY, splendidly, excellently, so as to become renowned; 1. 1. 35

FANE, temple; 1. 10. 20

FATIGATE, fatigued ('not post-Sh.', On.); 2. 2. 115

FAUCET, tap for drawing liquor from a barrel; 2. 1. 69

FAVOUR, countenance; 4. 3. 9

FEAR, (i) (*a*) fear for (w. 'person', (*b*) 'be afraid of' (w. 'ill report'); 1. 6. 69; (ii) fear for, distrust; 1. 7. 5

FEEBLE (vb.), disparage, depreciate; 1. 1. 194

FELLOWSHIP, 'for fellowship'= for company; 5. 3. 175

FETCH OFF, rescue; 1. 4. 63

FEVEROUS, afflicted with ague; 1. 4. 61

FIDIUS (vb.). Humorous coinage from 'Aufidius' (cf. 'fer', *H.V*, 4. 4. 29); 2. 1. 129

FIELD (sb.), (i) battle-field, campaign; 1. 2. 17; 'i' th' field', 'engaged in military operations'; 1. 9. 43; (ii) battle; 1. 7. 4; 1. 9. 33; 2. 2. 119

FIELDED, engaged in battle (cf. FIELD); 1. 4. 12

FILE, lit. '*Mil.* the number of men constituting the depth from front to rear of a formation in line' (O.E.D. 7), hence (i) rank; 5. 6. 34; (ii) 'the right-hand file'=those in the place of honour in the ranks (cf. *Sh. Eng.* I, 114), the best men, the patricians; 2. 1. 23; (iii) 'the common file'=the common herd; 1. 6. 43

FIND, (i) experience, feel; 5. 3. 111; (ii) understand, discover the truth; 3. 3. 129

FINE, punishment; 5. 6. 65

FIRE, 'fires of heaven'=stars (including sun and moon); 1. 4. 39

FIST (vb.), seize with the fist, i.e. try to throttle; 4. 5. 128

FIT (adj.), ready, prepared; 1. 3. 45

FIT (sb.), paroxysm of lunacy (app. Sh.'s special use; O.E.D. cites *Tit.* 4. 1. 17; *Err.* 4. 3. 88, and not again till Dryden, *Aeneid*, 1697); 3. 2. 33

FITLY, reasonably (iron.); 1. 1. 111

FIXED, unchanging; 2. 3. 249

FLAG, 'the bloody flag' was raised upon a declaration of war; 2. 1. 74

FLAMEN, ancient Roman priest, devoted to the service of a particular god; 2. 1. 210

FLAW, squall or gust of wind; 5. 3. 74

FLOURISH, a fanfare of trumpets, etc. to signalise the approach or entrance of a great or victorious person; 1. 9. 40 S.D., 66 S.D.; 2. 1. 154 S.D., 164 S.D., 202 S.D.; 2. 2. 152 S.D.; 5. 5. 7 S.D.

FLY OUT OF (itself), break out from its natural limits; 'depart from its own natural generosity' (J.); 1. 10. 19

FOB OFF (with), set aside by a trick (of); 1. 1. 93

FOIL (vb.), overcome, defeat; 1. 9. 48

FOLD IN, extend around, envelop; 3. 3. 68; 5. 6. 125

FOND, foolish; 4. 1. 26; 'fond of' wishing for; 5. 3. 162

FOOLERY, foolishness, foolhardiness; 3. 1. 245

FORCE, press, urge; 3. 2. 51

'FORE ME, mod. 'upon my soul'; 1. 1. 119

FORM, (i) formality; 2. 2. 142; (ii) formal, regular, procedure; 3. 1. 323

FOXSHIP. A coined variant of 'worship' as a title; the fox being the type of cunning and ingratitude; 4. 2. 18

FRAGMENT, sc. of a man (cf. *Troil.* 5. 1. 9); 1. 1. 221

FRANK, liberal; 3. 1. 130

FREE, (i) frank, unrestrained, undisguised; 2. 3. 199; 3. 3. 73; 5. 6. 26; (ii) generous; 3. 2. 88

FREE (vb.), absolve (cf. *Lucr.* 1208; *Wint.* 3. 2. 112); 4. 7. 47

FRIENDLY (adv.), in a friendly, peaceable way; 4. 6. 9

FROM, contrary to, divergent from; 3. 1. 90

FRONT (vb.), meet, confront, oppose; 5. 2. 41

FUNCTION, occupation, job; 4. 5. 34

FUSTY, (a) musty, mouldy, (b) smelly, ill-smelling; 1. 9. 7

GALEN, famous Greek physician, c. 130–199 A.D. (here an anachronism, like Cato, q.v.); 2. 1. 114

GALL (vb.), orig. 'make sore by chafing', hence, irritate, annoy; 2. 3. 194

'GAN, past tense of "gin" = begin; 2. 2. 113

GARB, manner, behaviour; 4. 7. 44

GARLAND, fig. chief ornament, 'glory' (O.E.D. cites Spenser, *Ruins of Time*, 1591); 1. 1. 183; 1. 9. 60; 2. 2. 99

GENERAL, (i) common, collective; 1. 1. 131; 3. 1. 146; 5. 3. 6; (ii) belonging to the common people; 3. 2. 66

GENEROSITY, the nobility (<Lat. *generosus*, of noble birth); 1. 1. 210

GENTLE, (i) gentleman-like; 2. 3. 96; (ii) 'being gentle wounded' = bearing oneself like a gentleman when wounded; 4. 1. 8

GENTRY, rank by birth; 2. 1. 235; 3. 1. S.D. init., 144

GET, (i) beget; 1. 3. 34; (ii) 'g. off', escape; 2. 1. 126

GETTER, begetter; 4. 5. 230

GIDDY, empty-headed frivolous; 1. 1. 267

GLOSSARY

141

GILDED, golden coloured (cf. *Ant.* 1. 4. 62); 1. 3. 61

GIRD, sneer or scoff at; 1. 1. 255

GIVE, (i) 'g. out', announce, proclaim; 1. 1. 192; (ii) report, represent; 1. 9. 55; (iii) (of the mind) misgive, make to suspect; 4. 5. 153; (iv) 'give way' = give one scope, fall in with one's plan; 4. 4. 25; 5. 6. 32

GLASS, eye-ball; 3. 2. 117

GOD-DEN, good evening or good afternoon (as parting greeting); 2. 1. 91; (as welcome); 4. 6. 20, 21

GOOD, well-to-do (cf. *M.V.* 1. 3. 12); here a quibble; 1. 1. 16

GRACE (sb.), (i) favour; 5. 3. 121; (ii) charm, elegance; 5. 3. 150

GRACE (vb.), (i) (*a*) show favour to, (*b*) embellish, adorn (cf. *L.L.L.* 5. 2. 72); 1. 1. 263; (ii) show favour to; 5. 3. 15

GRACIOUS, lovely; 2. 1. 173

GRAFT, fix graft on (a stock); 2. 1. 187

GRAINED, close-grained, tough, or showing the grain, rough; 4. 5. 111

GRATIFY, reward; 2. 2. 38

GRIEF-SHOT, sorrow-stricken; 5. 1. 44

GROAT, four-penny piece; 3. 2. 10

GUARD, custody or protection; 1. 10. 26

GUARDANT, 'Jack guardant'; *v.* JACK; 5. 2. 61

GUESS, think (cf. mod. American Eng.); 1. 1. 18

GUIDER, guide; 1. 7. 7

GULF, whirlpool (cf. *Ham.* 3. 3. 16) or bottomless pit (e.g. hell) that sucks down everything nearby (cf. 'sink', 1. 1. 121); 1. 1. 97; 3. 2. 91

HA. Excl. of surprise, joy, indignation, etc. (or simply interrog. = eh?); 2. 1. 100; 3. 1. 25; 5. 3. 19

HABITS, clothes, dress; 5. 3. 21 S.D.

HAND, 'in someone's hand' = led by someone; 5. 3. 23

HANDKERCHER, handkerchief (sp. 6 times, but 'handkerchief' a commoner Sh. sp.); 2. 1. 261

HAP (vb.), happen; 3. 3. 24

HASTY, rash, quick-acting (cf. *R.J.* 5. 1. 64; *K. John*, 4. 3. 97, 'thy hasty spleen'); 2. 1. 49

HAUTBOY, oboe, 'a wooden double-reed wind instrument of high pitch' (*Sh. Eng.*); 5. 4. 48 S.D.

HAVE, 'h. with you' = mod. coll. 'I'm with you!'. Common in Sh.; 2. 1. 267

HAVER, possessor; 2. 2. 83

HAVOC, merciless slaughter; 'cry "havoc"' = cry 'no quarter'. Orig. = give an army the signal for pillaging. But also a hunting-term; 3. 1. 273

HAZARD, game of dice with highly complicated chances; 'put in h.' = take the risk of; 2. 3. 255

HEAD, 'make a head' = gather together an army, raise an armed force; 2. 2. 86; 3. 1. 1

HEART. Regarded as the seat of wisdom as well as courage; 1. 1. 115, 135, etc.; 'h. of hope' here=person on whom all one's hopes are centred or depend; 1. 6. 55

HEAVY, heavy at heart, sad; 2. 1. 182; 4. 2. 48

HECTOR, chief Trojan hero in the *Iliad*; 1. 3. 42

HECUBA, Hector's mother, wife of Priam, King of Troy; 1. 3. 41

HELM, steersman, here fig., one who guides the affairs of the state; 1. 1. 76

HELP, remedy; 3. 1. 220

HOB, by-form of 'Rob', used generically for a rustic; 2. 3. 115

HOLD, keep, preserve; 2. 1. 237

HOLD! stop! (as an excl.); 5. 6. 132

HOLLOA (vb.), chase and holloa after; 1. 8. 7

HOLP, helped; 3. 1. 275; 4. 6. 82; 5. 3. 63; 5. 6. 36

HOME (adv.), (i) to the goal aimed at; so here, right into the enemy forces; 1. 4. 38; (ii) fully, plainly, thoroughly, effectively; 2. 2. 101; 3. 3. 1; 4. 1. 8, etc.

HONEST, upright, honourable; 1. 1. 54, 61; 2. 3. 132; 5. 3. 166

HOO! excl. of joy; 2. 1. 104; 3. 3. 137

HORSE (vb.), sit as on a horse, bestride; 2. 1. 208

HORSE-DRENCH, *v.* DRENCH; 2. 1. 116

HOSTILIUS, legendary king of Rome, second after Romulus, 2. 3. 239

HOUSEKEEPER, (a) one who stays at home, (b) woman engaged in domestic occupations; 1. 3. 52

HOW! what! 3. 1. 47, 75; 3. 3. 67; 4. 6. 122; 5. 2. 78

HUM. An interj. expressing dissent or dissatisfaction (cf. O.E.D. vb. 2); 5. 4. 22

HUM (vb.), greet with a 'hum' (*q.v.*); 5. 1. 49

HUMANELY, out of kindness of heart; 1. 1. 19

HUMOROUS, capricious, whimsical; 2. 1. 46

HUNGRY, unfertile, barren (O.E.D. 6), or 'eager for shipwrecks' (Mal.; cf. *Tw. Nt.* 2. 4. 100); 5. 3. 58

HUSBANDRY, careful, profitable management; 4. 7. 22

HUSWIFE, housewife; 1. 3. 71

HYDRA, many-headed monster slain by Hercules; as soon as he struck off one head two new ones grew; 3. 1. 93

IGNORANT. Either (i) unconscious (cf. *Tp.* 5. 1. 67) or (ii) stupid, simple (cf. *Meas.* 2. 4. 74, etc.); 2. 3. 173

IN, into; 2. 3. 257; 3. 1. 33, 96; 'to be in' (*v.* BE); 3. 2. 64

INCH, 'death by inches'=a lingering death; 5. 4. 39

INCLINE (to), side (with); 2. 3. 37

INDIFFERENTLY, neutrally; 2. 2. 16

INFECT, taint, deprave; 2. 1. 92

INFECTION, moral contamination (O.E.D. 6); 3. 1. 308

INFORM (trans. vb.), (i) make known, tell; 1. 6. 42; (ii) inspire, animate; 5. 3. 71

INGRATE, ungrateful; 5. 2. 83

INGRATEFUL, ungrateful; 2. 2. 30; 2. 3. 10

INHERENT, permanently fixed; 3. 2. 123

INHERIT, enjoy the possession of (cf. *Rom.* 1. 2. 30); 2. 1. 196

INHERITANCE, gaining possession of; 3. 2. 68

INJURIOUS, insulting; 3. 3. 69

INNOVATOR, revolutionary. 'Innovation' = 'revolution' elsw. in Sh.; change in civil affairs being in that age considered an evil; 3. 1. 174

INSINUATING, ingratiating; 2. 3. 98

INSTANT, immediate, here=got together at a moment's notice; 5. 1. 37

INSTRUMENT, organ (of the body); 1. 1. 100

INTEGRITY, organic unity; 3. 1. 159

INTERIM, 'by interims'=at intervals; 1. 6. 5

INTERJOIN, join reciprocally, unite; 4. 4. 22

INTERPRETATION, development (of a theme); 5. 3. 69

INVENTORY, a priced list of goods (cf. O.E.D. 1); 1. 1. 21

IRON, sword or dagger; 1. 5. 6

ISSUE, action (O.E.D. 8 b, 'rare', citing *J.C.* 3. 1. 295; *Cymb.* 2. 1. 51; cf. also *Meas.* 1. 1. 36); or poss. offspring (Rolfe); 4. 4. 22

ITHACA, island in the Aegean Sea, the domain of Ulysses; 1. 3. 85

JACK. Contemptuous term; 'Jack guardant'=fellow on guard; 5. 2. 61

JUDGEMENT, the administration of justice; 3. 1. 158

JUDICIOUS, ?judicial (cf. *Lear*, 3. 4. 76); 'meaning doubtful in' these two exx. (O.E.D.); 5. 6. 127. (N.B. 'judicial' non-Sh.)

JUMP, take risks for, i.e. 'by extension, apply a desperate remedy to' (On.); 3. 1. 154

JUNO, wife of Jupiter, given to anger; 2. 1. 99; 4. 2. 53

KAM (<Welsh *cam*), askew, awry (not again Sh.); 3. 1. 302

KNEE, walk kneeling; 5. 1. 5

LA. Excl. to call attention to, or emphasize, a statement; 1. 3. 68, 90

LAPSE, (*a*) glide, drop (of liquid), (*b*) fall into sin; 5. 2. 19

LEAD, flat lead-covered roof; 2. 1. 208; 4. 6. 83

LEASING, falsehood, lie; 5. 2. 22

LEG, obeisance by drawing back one leg, and bending the other; 2. 1. 68

LESSON (vb.), teach, instruct, admonish; 2. 3. 176

LET GO, let it be, say no more; 3. 2. 18

LETTERS, letter (pl. for sing.); 2. 1. 132

LEVY, 'the action for enrolling ...men for war' (O.E.D. 1*b*); 5. 6. 67

LIBERTY, right, privileges; 2. 3. 179, 214

LICTOR, Roman functionary, who walked before the magistrates carrying the *fasces*, a bundle of rods fastened with a strap round an axe; 2. 2. 34 S.D.

LIE, (i) 'lie in', i.e. for childbirth; 1. 3. 78; (ii) 'lie on', be incumbent on; 3. 2. 52

LIGHT, light-hearted, cheerful, merry; 2. 1. 182

LIGHTLY, thoughtlessly; 4. 1. 29

LIKE, likely; 1. 1. 192; 1. 3. 13; 2. 1. 238, etc.

LIKING, 'in their liking' = in favour with them; 1. 1. 194

LIMITATION, appointed time; 2. 3. 137

LIP, 'make a lip at' = despise (cf. *Wint.* 1. 2. 373, 'falling a lip of much contempt'); 2. 1. 113

LIST (vb.[1]), please, wish; 3. 2. 128

LIST (vb.[2]), hearken; 1. 4. 20; 3. 3. 40

LITTER (vb.), bring forth young (of animals); 3. 1. 238

LOCKRAM, 'a loosely woven fabric of hemp...used by lower-class persons for ruffs', coifs, etc. (Linthicum, 99–100); 2. 1. 206

'LONG, belong; 5. 3. 170

'LONG OF, because of; 5. 4. 29

LOOK, promise, look like. The only ex. in O.E.D. (8*b*) an extension of 'tend, point in a particular direction' (8*a*); 3. 3. 29

LOSE BY, throw away on (Schmidt.); 2. 3. 57

LOT, prize ticket in a lottery, 'lots to blanks' = a thousand to one; 5. 2. 10

LOVER, dear friend; 5. 2. 14

LURCH (vb.), (*a*) cheat, rob (O.E.D. vb.[1] 2); (*b*) to gain an easy and sweeping victory at cards, etc. (*v.* O.E.D. sb.[1] 2); 2. 2. 99

LYCURGUS, legendary wise lawgiver of Sparta; 2. 1. 54

MAGISTRATE, public functionary; 2. 1. 43; 3. 1. 104; 3. 1. 201

MAIM, 'mutilation or loss of some essential part' (O.E.D.); 4. 5. 89

MAKE, (i) represent as, make out to be; 1. 1. 174; (ii) 'make good' = secure, make sure of (mil. *v.* O.E.D. 'good', 22*d*); 1. 5. 12; (iii) 'make a hand' = make a success (of); 4. 6. 118; (iv) (with 'head' or 'the army'), muster, raise; 2. 2. 86; 3. 1. 1; 5. 1. 37

MALICE, malicious act; 2. 2. 31

MALKIN, untidy female, esp. servant, slut (dimin. of Malde = Matilda, Maud); 2. 1. 205

MAMMOCK, tear into fragments (cf. E.D.D. 'mammock' (sb.), scrap, broken piece—esp. of food); 1. 3. 66

MAN-ENTERED, initiated into manhood (O.E.D. 'man' 20; only ex.); 2. 2. 97

MANGLE, fig. mutilate, impair (cf. O.E.D. 3); 3. 1. 158

MANHOOD, courage; 3. 1. 245

MANKIND (adj.), (*a*) mad, frenzied (of diff. origin from (*b*), cf. O.E.D. *a*²); (*b*) human; 4. 2. 16

MAP, 'fig. A detailed representation in epitome. Very common in the 17th c.' (O.E.D. 2); 2. 1. 61

MARK, limit aimed at; 2. 2. 87

MARS, Roman god of war; 1. 4. 10; 4. 5. 121, 198

MASTERSHIP, masterly skill; 4. 1. 7

MATCH, bargain; 2. 3. 80

MATTER, 'no m. for that', that doesn't matter; 4. 5. 169

MATURE, ripe, ready, fully developed; 4. 3. 25

MAY, *v.* YOU MAY; 2. 3. 34

MEAN (vb. trans.), purpose, design; 1. 9. 57

MEASLE, scab, 'scurvy wretch' (On.). The word looks back both to O.F. *mesel*=leper, and to M.E. meseles=mod. 'measles'; the expr. 'why the meazils' (=pox! why, etc.) occurs in Jonson, *Barth. Fair*, 3. 4. 29; 3. 1. 78

MEASURE, 'with m.', commensurately, adequately; 2. 2. 121

MEDDLE, (i) busy oneself interferingly (with); 4. 5. 48; (ii) have sexual intercourse (with); 4. 5. 50

MEINY (orig.=household staff: cf. *Lr.* 2. 4. 35), 'the common herd' (O.E.D.); 3. 1. 66

MEMORY, memorial; 4. 5. 74; 5. 1. 17

MERCENARY, earning pay like a mere hired soldier; 5. 6. 41

MERCY, 'at mercy'='(that has surrounded) at discretion; absolutely in the power of the victor' (O.E.D. 5*b*); 1. 10. 7

MERELY, utterly; 3. 1. 303

MERIT (abs.), deserve well; 1. 1. 275

MICROCOSM, individual man (considered as a world or universe ('macrocosm') in miniature; 2. 1. 61

MIND, remind (cf. *H. V*, 4, 3, 13); 5. 1. 18

MINNOW, type of extreme insignificance (cf. *L.L.L.* 1. 1. 245); 3. 1. 89

MISERY, wretchedness (usual gloss), but poss.=avarice (Warb.); 2. 2. 125

MODEST, (i) chaste; 1. 1. 256; (ii) moderate, 'modest warrant'=authority to act with moderation; 3. 1. 274

MOE, more; 2. 3. 124; 4. 2. 21

MONSTER (vb.), declare wonderful beyond the bounds of nature; 2. 2. 75

MONSTROUS, unnatural; 2. 3. 9, 12

MORROW, morning (in 'good morrow'); 3. 3. 93

MORTAL, fatal; 2. 2. 109

MOTH, (*a*) mod. sense, (*b*) fig. parasite, idle person living at another's expense; 1. 3. 85

MOTION, (i) impulse, excitement, or (perhaps) motive; 2. 1. 50; (ii) prompting, influence; 2. 2. 51

MOULD, (i) bodily form (with quibble on 'mould'=earth); 3. 2. 103; (ii) matrix; 5. 3. 22

MOUNTEBANK (vb.), win like a quack at a fair, by tricking simpletons; 3. 2. 132

MOVE, make angry; 1. 1. 255

MOVER, person full of life and activity (cf. *Ven.* l. 368). Here ironical; 1. 5. 4

MUCH, 'make much of'=hold dear; 2. 3. 108

MULLED (from 'm. ale', sweetened and spiced ale), fig., dispirited, dull (On., Schmidt.); 4. 5. 230

MULTITUDINOUS, 'of or pertaining to a multitude' (O.E.D. cites no other ex.); 3. 1. 156

MUMMER, actor in a dumb-show; 2. 1. 73

MUNIMENTS, lit. fortifications; hence, 'furnishings' (O.E.D.) or 'defences' (O.E.D.); 1. 1. 117

MURRAIN, lit. a cattle plague (cf. *M.N.D.* 2. 1. 97); so, plague in general; 1. 5. 3

MUSE (vb.), wonder; 3. 2. 7

MUSTY, lit. 'mouldy'; here, fig., lethargic through want of practice (cf. O.E.D. 2*b*); 1. 1. 225

MUTINEER, rioter, rebel; 1. 1. 249

MUTINOUS, riotous, insurrectionary; 1. 1. 110, 148

MUTINY, popular rising; 2. 3. 255; 3. 1. 126, 228 S.D.

MUTUALLY, in common (now regarded as incorrect); 1. 1. 102

NAKED, unarmed; 1. 10. 20; 2. 2. 135

NAME, (i) honour, fame, repute (cf. *1 H. VI*, 4. 4. 9); 2. 1. 133; (ii) famous person; 4. 6. 126

NAPLESS, threadbare, with the nap worn off; 2. 1. 231

NATIVE (sb.), origin, what gives birth to; 3. 1. 129

NATURE, filial affection, natural ties; 5. 3. 25, 33

NAUGHT, lost, ruined (cf. *Ant.* 3. 10. 1); 3. 1. 230

NAVEL, fig. vulnerable centre; 3. 1. 123

NEPTUNE, god of the sea; 3. 1. 255

NERVE, sinew; 1. 1. 137

NERVY, sinewy (O.E.D. 1); 2. 1. 158

NICELY, scrupulously; 2. 1. 214

NIGHTLY, at night; 4. 5. 125

NOBLE (adj.), (*a*) mod. sense, (*b*) alchem. epithet for gold; 4. 1. 49

NOD, obeisance (ironical); 2. 3. 99

NOISE, music; here=military music; 2. 1. 157

NOSE (vb.), smell; 5. 1. 28

NOTHING (adv.), not at all; 1. 3. 100

NOTICE, observation; 2. 3. 156

NOTION, understanding; 5. 6. 107

Now, at one moment (folld. by 'straight'; cf. 'now...then', *3 H. VI*, 2. 5. 10; 'now...again', *A.Y.L.* 3. 2. 405); 3. 1. 34

NUMA, first of the legendary kings of Rome after Romulus; 2. 3. 238

NUMBER, company, (here) class; 3. 1. 72

OAK, oak-leaves. Actually the symbolic prize of a soldier who had rescued one taken prisoner in battle; but taken by Sh. as='garland', i.e. emblem of glory; 1. 3. 15; 2. 2. 96

OAKEN GARLAND (*v.* OAK); 2. 1. 123, 159 S.D.

OBJECT, spectacle (evoking pity or the opposite; cf. *Tim.* 4. 3. 123); 1. 1. 20

OBSTINATE, hard-hearted. Almost sinful; contrasted with 'constant'; 5. 3. 26

OCCASION, opportunity; 2. 1. 29

OCCUPATION, (i) handicraft; 4. 1. 14; (ii) manual workers (abstr. for concr.); 4. 6. 98

O'ERBEAR, overwhelm ('particularly of waters overwhelming the land', Schmidt; cf. *M.N.D.* 2. 1. 92; *Ham.* 4. 5. 102, etc.); 3. 1. 248; 4. 5. 134; 4. 6. 79

O'ERLEAP, omit; 2. 2. 134

O'ERPEER, look over, so as to be visible behind; 2. 3. 120

O'ERPRESSED, overwhelmed; 2. 2. 91

OF, (i) by; 2. 1. 22; 2. 2. 3; (ii) about; 2. 1. 70; 2. 2. 33; 4. 4. 17

OFF, beside the mark; 2. 2. 58

OFFENCE, offensive object; 5. 1. 28

OFFEND, annoy; 2. 1. 166

OFFER, (i) attempt; 2. 2. 64 S.D.; (ii) venture, dare, presume (cf. *Shr.* 5. 1. 60; *Tr.* 2. 3. 61); 5. 1. 23

OFFICE (sb.), (i) official duty; 3. 1. 35; (ii) inferior or outlying room of a house; 1. 1. 136

OFFICE (vb.), 'drive by virtue of one's office' (O.E.D.); 5. 2. 61

OFFICIOUS, offering or giving unwelcome help (cf. *M.N.D.* 3. 2. 330); 1. 8. 14

OLYMPUS, mt. at eastern end of range separating Thessaly and Greece proper; nearly 10,000 ft. high, seat of the gods in Greek mythology; hence type of very high mountain; 5. 3. 30

OMIT, neglect, disregard; 3. 1. 146

ONCE, once for all; 2. 3. 1

OPE (adj. and vb.), open; 1. 4. 43; 3. 1. 138; 5. 3. 183

OPINION, (i) self-conceit; 1. 1. 164; (ii) popular favour; 1. 1. 270

OPPOSER, antagonist, opponent; 1. 5. 22; 2. 2. 92; 4. 3. 35

OPPOSITE (sb.), adversary, opponent; 2. 2. 19

ORDINANCE, rank, order (only ex. cited in O.E.D.); 3. 2. 12

OSPREY, or Fish-hawk, large bird of prey, feeding on fish (*Pandion haliaetus*); 4. 7. 34

OSTENTATION, display, demonstration (of enthusiasm); 1. 6. 86

OTHER (adv.), otherwise; 4. 6. 103

OUT (adj.), forgetful of one's part (in acting); 5. 3. 41

OUT (adv.), outright (cf. *Tp.* 1. 2. 41); 4. 5. 124

OUT (prep.), out of; 5. 2. 39

OUT! (interj.), alas!; 5. 3. 24

OUTWARD, merely outward (show), not inward (reality); 1. 6. 77

OVERTA'EN, caught up with; so, fig. equalled; 1. 9. 19

OWE, (i) mod. sense; 2. 2. 131; (ii) be bound to pay for (nearly mod. sense); 3. 1. 241; (iii) possess (orig. sense); 5. 2. 80; 5. 6. 138 ('you'=for you);(iv) (a) owe (to yourself), (b) possess (as your own); 3. 2. 130

PACE, way of walking, gait; here, a term of the manage or riding-school (used fig.); 2. 3. 50

PAGE (fig.), attendant; 1. 5. 23

PAINFUL, arduous; 4. 5. 71

PALATE (vb.), taste, smack; 3. 1. 104

PALTERING, playing fast and loose, trickery; 3. 1. 58

PARCEL, part, portion; 1. 2. 32; 4. 5. 222

PART, (i) share; 1. 9. 39; (ii) side, party; 1. 10. 7; 5. 3. 121; so, 'upon the p.', on behalf (of); 3. 1. 209

PARTICULAR (adj.), individual, special; 5. 2. 67

PARTICULAR (sb.), (i) 'by particulars'=one by one; 2. 3. 42; (ii) 'for your particular' =as far as you are concerned; 4. 7. 13; (iii) 'in a dear particular'=very specially; 5. 1. 3

PARTICULARISE, lit. specify; and so, emphasize by contrast; 1. 1. 21

PARTY, (i) side, faction; 1. 1. 233; 3. 1. 313; 5. 2. 30; (ii) litigant (O.E.D. 11); 2. 1. 72; (iii) supporter, sharer; 5. 6. 14

PASS, (i) pass by, disregard; 2. 2. 137; 2. 3. 197; (ii) proceed; 3. 1. 53

PASSABLE, current. Quibbling on 'able to pass' (cf. *Cymb.* 1. 2. 10); 5. 2. 13

PASSING (adv.), exceedingly; 1. 1. 202

PATIENCE, 'by your patience', by your leave; 1. 3. 75; 1. 9. 55

PATIENT (adj.), long-suffering; 5. 6. 52

PAWN, stake, risk; 3. 1. 15; 5. 6. 21

PENELOPE, wife of Ulysses of Ithaca, who, pestered in his absence by parasite-suitors (l. 85, 'moths'), promised to choose one when she had finished the web she spun by day (and unravelled by night); 1. 3. 83

PEREMPTORY, determined (cf. *K.J.* 2. 1. 454); 3. 1. 284

PERFECT, accomplished; 2. 1. 80

PERSON, personal appearance, bearing, or behaviour; 1. 3. 10; 3. 2. 86

PESTER, infest; 4. 6. 7

PETITIONARY, suppliant; 5. 2. 74

PHYSIC, medical treatment of any kind; 3. 1. 154

PHYSICAL, good for the health; 1. 5. 18

PICK, pitch, toss; 1. 1. 199

PIECE (sb.), coin; 3. 3. 32

PIECE (vb.), lit. add pieces to, patch (shoe, garment), hence, augment, eke out (cf. *Ant.* 1. 5. 45; *H. V,* 1. Pr. 23); 2. 3. 211

PIERCING, affecting painfully, distressing; 1. 1. 82

PIKE, (*a*) lance (the chief weapon of the infantry), (*b*) pitch-fork; 1. 1. 23

PIN (vb.), fig. bolt; 1. 4. 18

PINCH (vb.), gripe, afflict with colic pains; 2. 1. 73

PLAINLY, 'without concealment or disguise' (O.E.D.); 5. 3. 3

PLANT, fix, establish firmly; 2. 2. 27

PLEBEII, plebeians; 2. 3. 183

PLOT, piece of earth; here, fig. single person (cf. MOULD); 3. 2. 102

PLUTO, god ruling Hades; 1. 4. 36

POINT, (i) 'at point to', about to; 3. 1. 193; 5. 4. 61; (ii) detail, 'obeys his points' =obeys him in every point (On.); 4. 6. 126

POLICY, stratagem (in war), political cunning (in statecraft); 3. 2. 42; 3. 2. 48

POLL (sb.), (i) number of heads; 3. 1. 134; (ii) 'by the p.', by counting of heads; 3. 3. 10

POLL (vb.), lit. shear; fig. pillage, despoil; 4. 5. 208

POPULAR. [Contemptuous in Sh.] (i) 'Studious of the favour of the common people' (O.E.D. 5*a*); 2. 3. 100; (ii) plebeian, vulgar; 2. 1. 211; 3. 1. 106; 5. 2. 40

PORCH, portico, colonnade; 3. 1. 239

PORT, gate; 1. 7. 1; 5. 6. 6

PORTANCE, bearing, behaviour; 2. 3. 223

POSSESS, inform; 2. 1. 130

POST, messenger (lit. one riding post-haste), courier; 5. 6. 50

POSTURE, attitude, bearing; 2. 1. 218

POT, 'to the pot' (sc. cut in pieces like meat for cooking), to death, destruction; cf. mod. 'gone to pot'; 1. 4. 48

POTCH (vb.), thrust (at) (see O.E.D. 'poach') 'Survives in Warwickshire' (On.); 1. 10. 15

POTHER, turmoil; 2. 1. 215

POUND UP, shut up as in a pound (i.e. an enclosure for stray cattle); 1. 4. 17

POUT, look sullen; 5. 1. 52

POWER, (i) armed force, army; 1. 2. 9, 32; 1. 3. 99; 1. 6. 8; 4. 5. 122; 4. 6. 67; (ii) exercise of power, control; 2. 1. 243

PRACTICE, plot, trickery; 4. 1. 33

PRANK (ref. vb.), lit. dress oneself up (or 'out'), here fig.; 3. 1. 23

PRECIPITATION, (i) precipice (O.E.D. does not cite again till 1890); 3. 2. 4; (ii) being hurled down from a height (the regular meaning); 3. 3. 102

PREPARATION, force equipped for battle; 1. 2. 15

PRESENT (sb.), 'the (this) present', the present time or occasion, 'the affair in hand' (On.); 1. 6. 60; 3. 3. 42

PRESENT (adj.), immediate; 3. 1. 211; 4. 3. 48

PRESENT (vb.), prescribe; 3. 2. 1

PRESENTLY, (i) mod. sense, rare in Sh.; 2. 3. 252; (ii) immediately (usu. sense in Sh.); 3. 3. 12; 4. 5. 220; 5. 6. 121

PRESS (vb.), impress, conscript; 1. 2. 9; 3. 1. 122

PRETENCE, intention, design; 1. 2. 20

PRETTY, pleasing; 1. 1. 89; 1. 3. 59

PRIVILEGE, right, claim; 1. 10. 24; 5. 3. 25

PROBABLE, 'worthy of belief', or 'capable of proof'; 4. 6. 66

PROCESS, regular course of law; 3. 1. 312

PROFESS, declare openly, affirm; 1. 3. 21

PROGENY, race, stock; here of progenitors, ancestors, not descendants; 1. 8. 12

PROOF (adj.), lit. proved and tested (of armour), hence fig. impervious (to fear); 1. 4. 25

PROPER, one's own; 1. 9. 57

PROPERLY, personally, for oneself; 5. 2. 81

PROSPERITY, success; 2. 1. 169

PROSPEROUS, successful; 2. 1. 102

PROSPEROUSLY, successfully; 5. 6. 75

PROUD, (a) (of animals) excitable, quarrelsome, lit. high-mettled, (b) (of warriors) valiant; 1. 1. 169

PROVAND, provender (here only in Sh.); 2. 1. 248

PROVE, try, put to the test; 1. 6. 62; 5. 1. 60

PSALTERY, 'ancient and medieval stringed instrument, more or less resembling the dulcimer, but played by plucking the strings with finger or plectrum' (Sh. Eng.); 5. 4. 49

PURCHASING, gaining, winning; 2. 1. 138

PURPOSE (sb.), proposal; 2. 2. 150; (vb.) resolve; 5. 3. 119

PURPOSED, intentional; 3. 1. 38

PUT, (i) 'put...to 't', force one to do one's utmost, press one hard; 1. 1. 228; 2. 2. 139; (ii) 'put forth', lit. bud, burgeon (cf. Ven. l. 416; H. V, 5. 2. 44; H. VIII, 3. 2. 352; O.E.D. 'put', 42g), so here, show promise, 'show fair blossom' (J.); 1. 1. 250; (iii) 'put upon, on', incite; 2. 1. 253; 2. 3. 251; (iv) 'put to that' =drive to such an extremity; 3. 1. 232

QUAKE, make tremble; 1. 9. 6

QUARRY, lit. heap of slain deer at the end of a chase; so, heap of dead men (cf. Macb. 4. 3. 206; Ham. 5. 2. 302); 1. 1. 197

QUARTERED, cut up (of a carcass); 1. 1. 198

QUESTION (vb.), doubt; 2. 1. 227

QUIT OF, 'even with by retaliation' (O.E.D.); 4. 5. 86

RAISE, originate a rumour (O.E.D. 14*b*); 4. 6. 70; 'raising' = originating a rumour; 4. 6. 61

RAKE, very lean person (quibble on the gardening tool); 1. 1. 23

RANGE (vb.), stretch out in a line (of buildings); 3. 1. 205

RANK-SCENTED, malodorous; 3. 1. 66

RAPT, transported, enraptured; 4. 5. 119

RAPTURE, fit, convulsions; 2. 1. 204

RARE, fine, splendid; 4. 5. 165

RASCAL, (*a*) one of a rabble, fellow of low birth, (*b*) lean, young, or inferior deer or other animal (here a hound); 1. 1. 158; 1. 6. 45

READ LECTURES (or lessons), give instruction (*v.* O.E.D. 11*b*); 2. 3. 234

REASON (sb.). Ellipt. = 'that's reasonable', 'there's good r. for it'; 4. 5. 236

REASON (vb.), (i) 'reason with', talk with, question; 4. 6. 52; (ii) support by argument (cf. *Lr.* 1. 2. 114); 5. 3. 176

RECEIPT, 'his receipt' = what was received by him; 1. 1. 111

RECOMMEND, consign, commit; 2. 2. 149

RECREANT, deserter, one who breaks allegiance; 5. 3. 114

RECTORSHIP, guidance, direction; 2. 3. 204

RED PESTILENCE. Perh. typhus (cf. *Tp.* 1. 2. 364); 4. 1. 13

REECHY, 'squalid, dirty' (O.E.D.); 2. 1. 206

REFUGE, resource; 5. 3. 11

REGARD, pay heed, pay attention; 3. 1. 67

REIN, rein in, restrain; 3. 3. 28

REJOURN, adjourn, put off; 2. 1. 70

RELISH, fig. flavour, smack, tincture (cf. *Ham.* 3. 3. 92, 'no relish of salvation in't'); 2. 1. 187

REMAIN (sb.), stay, 'make remain' = stay, remain (cf. *Macb.* 4. 3. 148); 1. 4. 63

REMEMBER, commemorate; 2. 2. 45

REMISSION, forgiveness; here prob. = authority to pardon; 5. 2. 81

REMOVE (sb.), raising of siege; 1. 2. 28

RENDER, give in return; 1. 9. 34

REPEAL (sb.), recall; 4. 1. 41

REPEAL (vb.), recall; 5. 5. 5

REPETITION, recital, mention; 1. 1. 45; 5. 3. 144

REPINE, complain, express dissatisfaction; 3. 1. 43

REPORT, reputation, good repute; 2. 1. 116; 2. 2. 27

REPOSE (reflex.), rest; 1. 9. 74

RE-QUICKEN, reanimate (O.E.D.); 2. 2. 115

REQUIRE, (i) make request of (a person); 2. 2. 154; (ii) ask for (something); 2. 3. 1

RESCUE, 'forcible taking of a person...out of legal custody' (O.E.D. 2); 3. 1. 275

RESPECT (sb.), regard, consideration; 3. 1. 180

RESPECT (vb.), pay heed to, (or) show respect for; 5. 3. 5

RESTRAIN, 'withhold, keep back; 5. 3. 167

RETIRE (sb.), retreat; 1. 6. 3

RETIRE (refl. or intrans. vb.), withdraw; 1. 3. 28; 1. 6. 50; 3. 1. 11

RETREAT (sb.), trumpet call to recall a pursuing force (O.E.D.; cf. 2 H. IV, 4. 3. 70); 1. 9. S.D. init.

REVEREND, worthy of reverence; 2. 1. 59; 2. 2. 40

RHEUM, lit. water secreted by glands; here contemptuous = tears; 5. 6. 46

RIDGE, 'the horizontal edge or line in which the two sloping sides of a roof meet at the top' (O.E.D.); 2. 1. 208

RIGHT, true; 2. 1. 233

ROAD, inroad, raid, incursion; 3. 1. 5

ROAR, utter loud cries of distress (cf. Schmidt); 4. 6. 125

ROTE (vb.), learn by heart; 3. 2. 55

ROTTEN, (i) mod. sense freq.; (ii) unwholesome (of fog, damp, etc.); 2. 3. 31; 3. 3. 121

RUB (sb.), check, obstacle (lit. obstruction or inequality on a bowling-green); 3. 1. 60

RUDELY, with violence; 4. 5. 146

RUTH, compassion; 1. 1. 196

SACKBUT, 'a bass trumpet, with a slide like that of a trombone for altering the pitch' (Sh. Eng.), now obsolete; 5. 4. 49

SAFEGUARD, guarantee of safe conduct; 3. 1. 9

SAFER, sounder; 2. 3. 217

SALT, i.e. tears; 5. 6. 93

SAUCE (vb.), spice, season; 1. 9. 53

SCAB, (a) mange, itch or other skin disease, (b) term of abuse ('scurvy' fellow); 1. 1. 165

SCALE (vb.), weigh, compare (cf. Meas. 3. 1. 253); 2. 3. 248

SCANDAL (vb.), slander, defame, or revile; 3. 1. 44

SCAPE (aphet. var.; freq. Sh.); escape; 1. 8. 13

SCONCE, (jocular) head; orig. = small fortification; 3. 2. 99

SCORN, (i) mock; 2. 3. 221; (ii) contemptuously refuse; 3. 1. 267

SCOTCH, gash (O.E.D. 4b, citing); 4. 5. 192

'SDEATH! Oath = 'God's (i.e. Christ's) death'; 1. 1. 216

SEAL, authenticate, confirm; 2. 3. 107

SEA-MARK. Conspicuous object for the direction of mariners set up by Trinity House, acc. to the act of 1566 (cf. Oth. 5. 2. 271); 5. 3. 74

SEASONED, (a) matured, (b) made palatable; 3. 3. 64

SECOND (sb.), supporter; 1. 4. 43; 1. 8. 15

SECOND (vb.), support (1); 4. 6. 63

SEEKING, object sought for; 1. 1. 187

GLOSSARY

SELD-SHOWN, seldom seen; 2. 1. 210

SENNET (prob. <signet=sign), notes on a trumpet or cornet for the entrance of a procession. App. a theatrical term only; 2. 1. 159 S.D.

SENSELESS, incapable of feeling; 1. 4. 54

SENSIBLE, sensitive; 1. 3. 86

SENSIBLY, i.e. with his sensitive body; 1. 4. 54

SENTENCE (vb.) pronounce as judgment, 'decree judicially'; 3. 3. 22

SERVANT (vb.), 'put in subjection to' (O.E.D.); 5. 2. 80

SET, (i) 'set down'; (α) encamp; 1. 2. 28; 1. 3. 100; 5. 3. 2; (β) trans. put down (in a time-table of duties), appoint; 1. 7. 2; (ii) 'set up' (of a top), start spinning, lit. get something going; 4. 5. 156

SEVERAL, separate, different; 1. 1. 184; 4. 5. 125; 4. 6. 39

SHAME (vb.), be ashamed; 2. 2. 65

SHENT (ppl. of 'shend'), reproached, rebuked; 5. 2. 95

SHOP, workshop, factory; 1. 1. 132

SHOUT FORTH, acclaim; 1. 9. 50

SHOW (sb.), indication; 3. 3. 36

SHOW (vb.), appear, seem; 3. 1. 126; 4. 6. 115; 5. 3. 13, 70

SHUNLESS, unshunnable; 2. 2. 110

SIDE (vb.), take sides with; 1. 1. 192

SINEWS, strength, lit. nerves; 5. 6. 45

SINGLE, (i) (a) solitary, (b) feeble (cf. *Macb.* 1. 3. 140; 1. 6. 16)); 2. 1. 36; (ii) individual, separate; 2. 3. 43

SINGLY, by any other single person; 2. 2. 85

SINGULARITY, individual, distinctive character (e.g. his insolence); 'more than his s.' =apart from his s.' (On.); 1. 1. 277

SINK, cesspool, sewer (cf. *Troil.* 5. 1. 73); 1. 1. 121

SIRRAH. Address to an inferior or to a child; 5. 2. 50; 5. 3. 75

SITHENCE, since; 3. 1. 47

SIT DOWN, begin a siege; 4. 7. 28

SLIGHT, of little worth, insignificant; 5. 2. 100

SLIGHTNESS, triviality; 3. 1. 148

SLIP, i.e. slip the leash; 1. 6. 39

SLIPPERY, uncertain, unstable; 4. 4. 12

SMOKING, reeking (with blood); 1. 4. 11

SOFT, gentle; 3. 2. 82

SOFT! (excl.), stop! 1. 1. 49

SOFT-CONSCIENCED, sloppy-minded; 1. 1. 36

SOMETHING (adv.), somewhat; 2. 1. 48; 2. 3. 82; 3. 2. 25

SOOTHE, flatter; 2. 2. 71; 3. 1. 69

SOOTHING, flattery; 1. 9. 44

SORT, (i) manner; 1. 3. 2; 4. 5. 232; (ii) class of people; 4. 6. 70

SOURLY, disagreeably; 5. 3. 13

SOUTH, i.e. S. wind, thought of as bringing fogs and pestilence; 1. 4. 30

GLOSSARY

SOVEREIGN, excellent, paramount; 2. 1. 114

SOWL, lug by the ears; 4. 5. 206

SPEAK, tell of, report; 2. 2. 101

SPECTATORSHIP (in), =for spectators to enjoy; 5. 2. 64

SPEND, give vent to, utter (On.); 2. 1. 52

SPICE, touch or trace, tincture; 4. 7. 46

SPIRE, summit; 1. 9. 24

SPOIL, (i) ravage; 2. 1. 214; (ii) slaughter, massacre (esp. of deer; cf. *Caes.* 3. 1. 207); 2. 2. 118; (iii) (plur.) plunder, booty; 2. 2. 122

SPOT, an embroidered pattern of small flowers, fruits, etc. (cf. Linthicum, p. 148); 1. 3. 53

SPRIGHTLY, spirited, lively, brisk; 4. 5. 228

STAIN (sb.), overshadowing, eclipse, disgrace; 1. 10. 18

STALE (vb.), make stale; 1. 1. 91

STAMP (sb.), (i) distinguishing mark, characteristic; 1. 6. 23; (ii) tool for stamping a mark, figure, design or the like, upon a softer material (O.E.D. 5); 2. 2. 105

STAMP (vb.), lit. coin, hence, pass into currency; 5. 2. 22

STAND, (i) stand fast (int.); 5. 3. 35; withstand (trans.); 5. 3. 74; (ii) stop; 5. 6. 127; (iii) 'stand out', refuse to take part; 1. 1. 240; (iv) 'stand for', (α) defend, support; 2. 2. 39; (β) be a candidate for; 2. 3. 186; (v) 'stand upon' or 'on', insist on; 2. 2. 148; 4. 6. 87; (vi) 'stand up', make a stand;

2. 3. 14; (vii) 'stand with', agree, be consistent with; 2. 3. 84; (viii) 'stand to', uphold, support; 3. 1. 207; 5. 3. 199; (ix) 'stand to 't', fight stoutly; 4. 6. 10

STATE, (i) government; 1. 1. 68, 76; (ii) chair of state or throne; 5. 4. 23

STAY, (i) 'stay behind', fail to take part in; 1. 1. 240; (ii) 'stay upon', wait for; 5. 4. 7–8

STEM, prow of a ship or boat; 2. 2. 105

STICK (vb.), (i) be fixed as an ornament; 1. 1. 270; (ii) hesitate; 2. 3. 15; (iii) stand out and stand fast; 5. 3. 73

STILL (adj.), silent, quiet; 3. 2. 11; 4. 6. 37

STILL (adv.), always, constantly; 1. 1. 99, etc.

STIR, become excited; here prob., make a commotion, rise in revolt; 3. 1. 53

STOUTNESS, overbearing arrogance or obstinacy; 3. 2. 127; 5. 6. 27

STRAINS, 'the fine strains'= the refinements; 5. 3. 149

STRAIGHT, immediately; 2. 2. 114; 2. 3. 146; 3. 1. 35; 3. 3. 25; 4. 5. 90

STRETCH, STRETCH OUT, strain to the utmost; 2. 2. 49; 5. 6. 45

STRIKE, (i) fight, lit. wield a weapon (cf. *Ant.* 3. 8. 3; *H. V*, 2. 4. 54); 1. 6. 4; (ii) blast, destroy. 'Astrol. term: by the influence of planets in opposition'; 2. 2. 111

STRUCKEN, struck; 4. 5. 153

SUBDUE, subject to punishment (On.); 1. 1. 174

SUBJECT, 'creature, being; that which is in existence' (Schmidt); 2. 1. 83

SUBTLE, (i) crafty; 1. 10. 17; (ii) 'tricky', 'deceptively smooth' (G.G.); 5. 2. 20

SUCCESS, (i) fortune, result of action (good or bad); 1. 1. 259; 1. 6. 7; 5. 1. 62; (ii) mod. sense; 2. 2. 42

SUDDEN, (i) 'on the sudden', very quickly (O.E.D. 'very common c. 1560–1700'); 2. 1. 218; (ii) hasty, done on the spur of the moment; 2. 3. 250

SUFFER, allow; 3. 1. 40

SUFFERANCE, suffering, distress; 1. 1. 22

SUFFRAGE, vote; 2. 2. 136

SUGGEST, (tr.) 'insinuate'; 2. 1. 242; (intr.); 2. 1. 250

SUMMON, call to surrender; 1. 4. 7

SUPPLE, compliant; 2. 2. 25

SURCEASE, cease; 3. 2. 121

SURE, SURE ON'T (adv.), assuredly; 2. 3. 28; 3. 1. 271; 5. 1. 35

SURE (adj.), to be relied upon; 1. 1. 171

SURETY (vb.), stand surety for, go bail for; 3. 1. 177

SWAY (vb.), hold sway, rule; 2. 1. 201

SWORN BROTHER, most intimate friend. Lit. the 'frater juratus' of medieval chivalry, under oath to share another's fortunes (cf. Ado, 1. 1. 68; R. II, 5. 1. 20); 2. 3. 95

SYNOD, assembly; 5. 2. 67

TABLE, meal, banquet; 2. 1. 80

TABOR, 'a merry little side-drum' (G.G.); 1. 6. 25; 5. 4. 50

TACKLE, ship-rigging; 4. 5. 64

TA'EN FORTH, picked out, selected; 1. 9. 34

TAG, lit. odds and ends; here = rabble; 3. 1. 247

TAINT, sully, discredit; 4. 7. 38

TAKE, (i) take effect (i.e. kill); 2. 2. 106; (ii) destroy; 3. 1. 111; 4. 4. 20; (iii a) 'take up', take on (cf. 2 H. IV, 1. 3. 73); 3. 1. 243; (iii b) 'take up', fill up, obstruct (cf. H. VIII, 1. 1. 56); 3. 2. 116; (iv) 'take in', capture; 1. 2. 24; 3. 2. 59; (v) 'come upon unexpectedly' (Schmidt); 5. 1. 50

TARGET, shield, 'targe'; 4. 5. 123

TARPEIAN ROCK, rock on the Capitoline hill, from which traitors were hurled headlong; 3. 1. 212, 265; 3. 2. 3; 'Tarpeian death' = death thus brought about; 3. 3. 88

TARQUIN, Tarquinius Superbus, the younger of the two kings of this surname, expelled from Rome (Livy, Bk. 1); he was the violator of Lucretia, acc. to the story in Livy, the subject of Sh.'s Lucrece; and was defeated at L. Regillus, when endeavouring to recover his throne, c. 496 B.C.; 2. 1. 148; 2. 2. 92

TASK (vb.), set a task; 1. 3. 37

TASTE, (i) preference (with quibble on taste='flavour'); 'greatest taste'=the preference of the majority; 3. 1. 103; (ii) sample; 3. 1. 316

TAUNTINGLY, sneeringly, mockingly (cf. O.E.D. 'taunt', vb. 2); 1. 1. 109

TELL, 'canst thou tell?'=do you know?; 5. 2. 34

TEMPERANCE, self-control, restraint; 3. 3. 28

TENDER-BODIED, i.e. very young; 1. 3. 6

TENT (vb.¹), lit. apply a roll of lint to probe and cleanse a wound, hence, cure, heal; 1. 9. 31; 3. 1. 235

TENT (vb.²), lodge; 3. 2. 116

TETTER (vb.), affect with tetter (=a gen. term for skin eruption, cf. *Ham.* 1. 5. 71); 3. 1. 79

THEME, subject, discussion; 1. 1. 219; 2. 2. 55

THINK UPON, think kindly of (cf. *Ant.* 1. 5. 27), 'remember with compassion' (Beeching, citing Jonah i. 6); 2. 3. 55, 187

THOROUGH, through; 5. 3. 115

THREAD, pass through one after another; 3. 1. 124

THROAT, voice (cf. *Oth.* 3. 3. 357); 3. 2. 112

THRONE (vb.), be enthroned; 5. 4. 25

THROW, distance to which anything should be thrown; here a term in bowling; 5. 2. 21

TICKLE, gratify (cf. *K.J.* 2. 1. 583); 1. 1. 259

TIGER-FOOTED, 'fierce and swift' (On.); 3. 1. 310

TIME, (i) the present; 2. 1. 266; (ii) state of affairs; 2. 3. 118; 4. 1. 40; 4. 6. 27; (iii) one's contemporaries; 4. 7. 50; (iv) future ages (cf. *Son.* 18. 12); 5. 3. 127

TIME-PLEASER, time-server; 3. 1. 45

TINDER-LIKE, flaring up quickly; 2. 1. 49

To, (i) compared with, 'even to the altitude of his virtue', even when you take into account his exalted valour; 1. 1. 39; 2. 1. 115; (ii) in addition to; 2. 1. 162; (iii) '(pawn) to'=(stake) upon; 3. 1. 16

TOGE, toga; 2. 3. 114

TOP (vb.), surpass; 2. 1. 20

TOUCH (sb.), lit. the test for gold by a touchstone; hence, fig., stamp, quality ('of noble t.'; *v.* NOBLE); 4. 1. 49

TOUCH (vb.), (i) affect; 2. 1. 55; (ii) threaten (a fencing term); 3. 1. 123; 2. 1. 252; (iii) test; 2. 3. 190

TOUCHING, concerning; 1. 1. 151

TOWARDS, with, in dealing with; 5. 1. 41

TRADE, handicraft; so, workers; 3. 2. 134; 4. 1. 12

TRADUCEMENT, calumny; 1. 9. 22

TRANSLATE, transform; 2. 3. 188

TRANSPORT, (i) carry away by violent passion; 1. 1. 74; (ii) 'temperately transport' =control himself while he swears; 2. 1. 221

TREATY, proposal requiring ratification, negotiation; 2. 2. 53; 5. 6. 68

TRIBE, (i) Lat. *tribus.* The citizens were divided into political divisions called tribes; three for the patricians and thirty for the plebs; 3. 3. 11; (ii) race, perh. contemptuous 'pack'; 4. 2. 24; 5. 6. 129

TRIER, tester; 4. 1. 4

TRIM, =either (if sb.) trappings (cf. *Ant.* 4. 4. 22, where it=armour), or (if adj.) fine (*v.* BELONGING); 1. 9. 62

TRITON, a sea-god, Neptune's trumpeter; 3. 1. 89

TROOP, group of men, crowd (not of soldiers); 1. 1. 203

TROPHY, symbolic monument (gen. associated in Sh. with funerals; cf. *Ham.* 4. 5. 213); 1. 3. 41

TROTH, truth; 4. 5. 192; 'in troth', truly; 1. 3. 107; 2. 1. 135

TRUE (sb.), truth (O.E.D. sb.2); 5. 2. 32

TRY, test; 2. 3. 191; 3. 1. 224

TUMBLE (intr.), 'roll about on the ground' (O.E.D. 2); 5. 2. 21

TUNE, (*a*) humour, (*b*) tone; 2. 3. 85

TURN, bring (to a certain condition); 3. 1. 282; (ii) make to change, alter; 4. 6. 60

TWIN (vb.), be like twins (cf. *Per.* 5 Pr. 8); 4. 4. 15

TWIST, plaited thread (O.E.D.); 5. 6. 96

TYRANNY, cruelty, ruthlessness; 5. 3. 43

UNACTIVE, inactive; 1. 1. 98

UNAPT, not readily disposed; 5. 1. 52

UNBARBED, unarmed; 3. 2. 99

UNBUCKLE, tear off (in fight); 4. 5. 128

UNCLOG, disencumber, relieve of a load; 4. 2. 47

UNDERCREST, wear as a family crest; 1. 9. 72

UNDO, destroy; 1. 1. 62, 63

UNGRAVELY, in an undignified manner, unbecoming one's dignity; 2. 3. 224

UNHEART, dishearten; 5. 1. 49

UNKNIT, fig. untie; 4. 2. 31

UNLIKE, unlikely; 3. 1. 48

UNPROPERLY, unfittingly, contrary to propriety; 5. 3. 54

UNSCANNED, unconsidered, inconsiderate; 3. 1. 311

UNVULNERABLE, invulnerable; 5. 3. 73

UP, in a position of influence or power; 3. 1. 109

UPHOLD, assist, support; 1. 9. 40

UPON, (i) on the ground of; 2. 1. 225; (ii) for the purpose of, about; 2. 3. 143

USE, treat; 2. 2. 153; 2. 3. 161; 5. 2. 51

USED, wont, customary to be done; 3. 1. 114

USHER, 'a male attendant on a lady' (O.E.D. 2*b*); 1. 3. 48 S.D.

VAIL, lower (in reverence); 3. 1. 98

VALUE (sb.), estimate; 2. 2. 57

VANTAGE, (i) advantage, profit; 1. 1. 159; 2. 3. 259; 3. 2. 31; (ii) opportunity, advantageous moment; 5. 6. 54

VARIABLE, diverse, varying; 2. 1. 209

*VARNISH, lit. put a fresh gloss upon, (of persons) represent in the most favourable light, lay it on thick with (cf. *Ham.* 4. 7. 133); 5. 2. 17

VASSAL, slave; 3. 2. 9

VAWARD, vanguard; 1. 6. 53

VENGEANCE (adv.), mod. slang. 'mortally', 'with a vengeance'; 2. 2. 5

VENT (sb.). Meaning doubtful; 'full of vent' either = full of sport or excitement (<vent=the scent of an animal in the chase) or = bursting with life, providing plenty of outlet for activity of all kinds (<vent=discharge or outlet, e.g. from a cask, in contrast to 'mulled'); 4. 5. 229

VENT (vb.), (i) void, get rid of; 1. 1. 224; (ii) utter; 3. 1. 257

VEXATION, mortification, torment (of mind); 3. 3. 140

VIAND, food; 1. 1. 99

VIPEROUS, venomous, poisonous (fig.); 3. 1. 285

VIRGIN, 'virgin it', remain chaste; 5. 3. 48

VIRGINAL, maidenly; 5. 2. 43

VIRTUE, (i) valour; 1. 1. 39; (ii) power, efficacy; 5. 2. 12

VOICE (sb.), (i) vote; 2. 2. 138; 2. 3. 1, 35, 44, etc.; (ii) voter; 2. 3. 124, 210; 3. 3. 9; 4. 6. 147

VOICE (vb.), nominate, elect; 2. 3. 233

VOUCH (sb.), attestation, formal confirmation; 2. 3. 116

VOUCH (vb.), affirm, guarantee (a statement); 1. 9. 24; 5. 6. 5

VULGAR, (i) of the common people, plebeian; 1. 1. 215; 4. 7. 21; (ii) among the plebeians; 2. 1. 212

WAGE, hire (as a mercenary); 5. 6. 40

WANTON, (a) unrestrained, (b) lascivious (fig.); 2. 1. 214

WATCH, lie awake, keep watch (as a soldier); 2. 3. 126

WAVE, waver (O.E.D. 3); 2. 2. 16

WAY, scope, freedom of action (cf. GIVE); 4. 4. 25; 5. 6. 32

WEALSMAN, 'one devoted to the public weal; commonwealth's man' (O.E.D.); 2. 1. 53

WEED, sing. and pl., clothes, apparel; 2. 3. 152, 220

WEIGH, 'be of (much or little) value or account' (O.E.D.); 'as they weigh' = according to their worth; 2. 2. 72

WELL-FOUND, 'commendable, well-approved' (O.E.D., citing also *All's*, 2. 1. 102); poss. = welcome (cf. O.E.D. 1); 2. 2. 42

WHAT, why; 3. 1. 315

WHERE, whereas; 1. 10. 13

WHIP, fig. scourge; 1. 8. 12

WHOLESOME, (i) not mouldy; 1. 1. 18; (ii) salutary; 1. 1. 81; (iii) profitable; 2. 1. 68; (iv) seasonable (+a quibble on (ii)); 2. 3. 59

WHOOP OUT, drive out with derisive cries; 4. 5. 81

WIN UPON, get the better of (or) encroach upon (O.E.D. 10); 1. 1. 220

WIND (vb.), refl., insinuate oneself (into); 3. 3. 64

WITH 'be with them'=get round them with, play this little trick on them (cf. *Wint.* 4. 3. 116); 3. 2. 74

WOLVISH, like a wolf. Doubtful relevance; poss.=simply 'rough, shaggy' (E.K.C.); 2. 3. 114

WOOLLEN, clad in woollen clothing, a 'mark of lowly status' (O.E.D.); 3. 2. 9

WORD, 'at a word'=in short; 1. 3. 110

WORN, enfeebled, exhausted; 3. 1. 6

WORSHIP, dignity, authority, sovereignty; 3. 1. 142

WORSHIPFUL, most honourable; 1. 1. 249

WORTH, 'full quota, due proportion' (Mal.); 3. 3. 26

WORTHY, deserving praise, heroic; 2. 2. 121; 'make worthy'=make a hero of; 1. 1. 174

WREAK (sb.), revenge (again *Tit.* 4. 3. 33); 4. 5. 88

WRENCH, twist forcibly; 1. 8. 11

YIELD, grant; 2. 2. 52

YOKE (with), be coupled (with), associated (with); 3. 1. 57

YOU MAY, =you may have your little joke; 2. 3. 34

YOUNGLY, in youth; 'how youngly'=in what extreme youth; 2. 3. 235

WORDSWORTH CLASSICS

General Editors: Marcus Clapham & Clive Reynard

JANE AUSTEN
Emma
Mansfield Park
Northanger Abbey
Persuasion
Pride and Prejudice
Sense and Sensibility

ARNOLD BENNETT
Anna of the Five Towns

R. D. BLACKMORE
Lorna Doone

ANNE BRONTË
Agnes Grey
The Tenant of
Wildfell Hall

CHARLOTTE BRONTË
Jane Eyre
The Professor
Shirley
Villette

EMILY BRONTË
Wuthering Heights

JOHN BUCHAN
Greenmantle
Mr Standfast
The Thirty-Nine Steps

SAMUEL BUTLER
The Way of All Flesh

LEWIS CARROLL
Alice in Wonderland

CERVANTES
Don Quixote

G. K. CHESTERTON
Father Brown:
Selected Stories
The Man who was
Thursday

ERSKINE CHILDERS
The Riddle of the Sands

JOHN CLELAND
Memoirs of a Woman of
Pleasure: Fanny Hill

WILKIE COLLINS
The Moonstone
The Woman in White

JOSEPH CONRAD
Heart of Darkness
Lord Jim
The Secret Agent

J. FENIMORE COOPER
The Last of the
Mohicans

STEPHEN CRANE
The Red Badge of
Courage

THOMAS DE QUINCEY
Confessions of an English
Opium Eater

DANIEL DEFOE
Moll Flanders
Robinson Crusoe

CHARLES DICKENS
Bleak House
David Copperfield
Great Expectations
Hard Times
Little Dorrit
Martin Chuzzlewit
Oliver Twist
Pickwick Papers
A Tale of Two Cities

BENJAMIN DISRAELI
Sybil

THEODOR DOSTOEVSKY
Crime and Punishment

SIR ARTHUR CONAN
DOYLE
The Adventures of
Sherlock Holmes
The Case-Book of
Sherlock Holmes
The Lost World &
Other Stories
The Return of
Sherlock Holmes
Sir Nigel

GEORGE DU MAURIER
Trilby

ALEXANDRE DUMAS
The Three Musketeers

MARIA EDGEWORTH
Castle Rackrent

GEORGE ELIOT
The Mill on the Floss
Middlemarch
Silas Marner

HENRY FIELDING
Tom Jones

F. SCOTT FITZGERALD
A Diamond as Big as the
Ritz & Other Stories
The Great Gatsby
Tender is the Night

GUSTAVE FLAUBERT
Madame Bovary

JOHN GALSWORTHY
In Chancery
The Man of Property
To Let

ELIZABETH GASKELL
Cranford
North and South

KENNETH GRAHAME
The Wind in the
Willows

GEORGE & WEEDON
GROSSMITH
Diary of a Nobody

RIDER HAGGARD
She

THOMAS HARDY
Far from the
Madding Crowd
The Mayor of Casterbridge
The Return of the
Native
Tess of the d'Urbervilles
The Trumpet Major
Under the Greenwood
Tree

Distribution

**AUSTRALIA
& PAPUA NEW GUINEA
Peribo Pty Ltd**
58 Beaumont Road, Mount Kuring-Gai
NSW 2080, Australia
Tel: (02) 457 0011 Fax: (02) 457 0022

**CZECH REPUBLIC
Bohemian Ventures spol s r o**
Delnicka 13, 170 00 Prague 7
Tel: 02 877837 Fax: 02 801498

**FRANCE
Chiron Diffusion**
40, Rue de Seine, Paris 75006,
Tel: 1 43 26 47 56 Fax: 1 45 83 54 61

**GREAT BRITAIN & IRELAND
Wordsworth Editions Ltd**
Cumberland House, Crib Street
Ware, Hertfordshire SG12 9ET

**SCOTLAND
Lomond Books**
36 West Shore Road, Granton
Edinburgh EH5 1QD

**INDIA
OM Book Service**
1690 First Floor
Nai Sarak, Delhi – 110006
Tel: 3279823-3265303 Fax: 3278091

**IRAN
World Book Distributers**
26 Behrooz Street, Suite 6
Tehran 19119
Tel: 9821 8714622 Fax: 9871 50044

**ISRAEL
Timmy Marketing Limited**
Israel Ben Zeev 12
Ramont Gimmel, Jerusalem
Tel: 02-865266 Fax: 02-880035

**ITALY
Magis Books SRL**
Via Raffaello 31/C
Zona Ind Mancasale
42100 Reggio Emilia
Tel: 1522 920999 Fax: 0522 920666

**NEW ZEALAND
Allphy Book Distributors Ltd**
4-6 Charles Street, Eden Terrace
Auckland,
Tel: (09) 3773096 Fax: (09) 3022770

**PHILIPPINES
I J Sagun Enterprises**
P O Box 4322 CPO Manila
2 Topaz Road, Greenheights Village
Taytay, Rizal
Tel: 631 80 61 TO 66

**PORTUGAL
International Publishing Services Ltd**
Rua da Cruz da Carreira, 4B,
1100 Lisbon
Tel: 01 570051 Fax: 01 3522066

**SINGAPORE,
MALASIA & BRUNEI
Paul & Elizabeth Book Services Pte Ltd**
163 Tanglin Road No 03-15/16
Tanglin Mall, Singapore 1024
Tel: (65) 735 7308 Fax: (65) 735 9747

**SLOVAK REPUBLIC
Slovak Ventures spol s r o**
Stefanikova 128, 94901 Nitra
Tel/Fax: 087 25105

**CYPRUS
Huckleberry Trading**
3 Othos Avvey, Tala Paphos
Tel: 06 653585

**SPAIN
Ribera Libros, S.L.**
Poligono Martiartu, Calle 1 - no 6
48480 Arrigorriaga, Vizcaya
Tel: 34 4 6713607 (Almacen)
     34 4 4418787 (Libreria)
Fax: 34 4 6713608 (Almacen)
     34 4 4418029 (Libreria)

**DIRECT MAIL
Redvers**
Redvers House
13 Fairmile, Henley-on-Thames
Oxfordshire RG9 2JR
Tel: 01491 572656 Fax: 01491 573 590